the daily 5

FOSTERING LITERACY INDEPENDENCE IN THE ELEMENTARY GRADES

GAIL BOUSHEY AND JOAN MOSER
"THE SISTERS"

Stenhouse Publishers
Portland, Maine

Stenhouse Publishers
www.stenhouse.com

Library of Congress Cataloging-in-Publication Data
Boushey, Gail, 1956–
The daily five : fostering literacy independence in the elementary grades / Gail Boushey and Joan Moser, "the sisters".
        p. cm.
Includes bibliographical references.
ISBN 1-57110-429-1
1. Language arts (Elementary) 2. Individualized instruction--Case studies. I. Moser, Joan, 1962– II. Title.

LB1576.B535 2006
372.6--dc22
        2005057497

Cover and interior design by Beth Caissie
Typeset by Beth Caissie

The Daily Five® and The Daily Cafe® are registered trademarks of The 2 Sisters, Joan Moser and Gail Boushey.

Manufactured in the United States of America on recycled paper with a 30% PCW content.
15 14 13 12 11   16 15

DEDICATION

■ ■ ■ ■ ■

Dedicated to
our husbands, Doug and Dean, for their unyielding support;
Jolie, Emily, and Madeline, who have inspired us each step of the way;
Marlene, who inspires us to be lifelong learners;
and
Dad, whose unconditional love and pride give us wings.

CONTENTS

■■■■■

ACKNOWLEDGMENTS

■ ■ ■ ■ ■

Many people have influenced our lives as educators, presenters, and authors. Recognizing every person who has helped and supported us through this project would lead to acknowledgments that were longer than the book itself. Although this is not a comprehensive record of them all, the following people have had a direct influence on our journey.

Margaret Mooney planted the first seed that there might be an alternative way to keep kids busy while we taught small groups and individuals. She pushed our thinking to create engaged and independent learners while feeding our teaching souls (and our stomachs).

Michael Grinder revolutionized our thinking. His voice and influence is infused throughout our work with children and throughout this book as well.

Regie Routman's influence has made our teaching and conferring with children more purposeful and meaningful.

Katy Brady was the first person to say, "Girls, you have got to write this in a book!"

Ben and Elaine Brady are friends and advocates who put actions behind their words of support.

Barbara Lawson placed opportunities in front of us.

Steven Layne's passion for children and literacy inspires us.

Troy Brown helped organize our thinking at this project's conception.

Sonja Ntamark contributed beautiful photographs.

Arlene Murphy helped us put words to paper.

Colleagues and class participants requested this book and asked tough questions that forced us to reflect on and refine all we do.

Philippa Stratton gave the initial nod to this project. All of the production folks at Stenhouse: Production Manager Jay Kilburn, copy editor Laurel Robinson, and designer Beth Caissie, your talents and efforts make our work the very best it can be!

Lori Sabo helped us say exactly what we wanted to, believes in the message as passionately as we do, and captured much of it on film.

And Brenda Power—this journey would have been impossible without you. Your kindness, incredible sense of humor, ability to understand the Daily Five, love of a good laugh, and office supplies made our work with you joyful. You are a guide, counselor, and encourager and will always be considered a friend. We couldn't have had a more perfect editor!

Jolie, Emily, and Madeline—let's take that trip.

Dean and Doug—we love you for your reflections and support. Thank you.

NOTE TO READERS

■■■■■■

The Daily Five is a structure that we have designed, taught, and refined together. Whether sitting in one of our conference sessions, classes, or joining us for a cup of coffee, you'd be struck by how united we are in our passion and approach to learning and literacy.

We use the term "we" throughout the book, not because we teach together, but because the way we structure learning and work with children is identical. The use of "we" isn't meant to be confusing, but is evidence that it wouldn't matter which of our classrooms you visited, you'd observe the same behaviors and hear the same language in both.

PART I

Daily Five Basics

01
INTRODUCTION

■■■■■

The typical teacher has children doing a lot of "stuff." How is what I am having children do creating readers and writers?

—*Regie Routman*

■■■■■

That was then. This is now.

When we were just starting out as teachers, we were critically aware of the challenges and joys ahead of us in our new profession. We heard about and experienced students such as Devon, who wanted to read but struggled to lift any word off the page; Emily, who devoured every chapter book conceivable for a third grader; and Nadezdah, who had just arrived in the United States and was beginning to learn English, but was not ready to speak. We learned about the standards that our school district and state mandated, along with the expectations of teachers to get all students to achieve them. Yet our knowledge was limited in terms of how to manage and instruct with this wide range of needs.

If you had walked into our classrooms during literacy time in our first years of teaching, you might have seen children who were sitting at their desks working on worksheets, or clustered at centers looking quite busy. Except for Jason—he was sharpening his pencil and bothering a group of students sitting nearby. At the same time, we had a group of four students in front of us ready for a reading lesson. We were working hard as we left the group, racing around trying to redirect Jason and help another student at centers. We headed back to sit with the group, and oops, there we went again, up and moving as we headed toward Katie, who was wandering aimlessly in the book area, disturbing the other children trying to work near her. Katie said she was looking for a book. Our brows furrowed as we tried to help Katie quickly find a book. We glanced back at the small group we had just left, who were no longer reading the section of the book we had asked them to read but instead were showing one another how they could make their armpits squeak. We headed back in the direction of the small group, redirecting a couple of children along the way. Our reading time was this daily frantic dance.

At the end of the day, we would dismiss our children and then slump wearily into the closest chair. We looked longingly at the beautiful weather outside, just calling to us for a long walk. But our eyes would fall upon the stacks of "things" our children had done during literacy time. Those things ranged from worksheets that went with the mandated district reading program to projects designed to "extend" stories for the week: book covers, dioramas, and posters with main-character faces. All of these items, and many more, were used to keep children busy while we attempted, none too successfully, to work with a few small groups and individuals. Because we had asked our children to do those "things," we certainly had to look at each one and at least make a mark on the paper. For the hundredth time we asked ourselves, "But did those things just keep our kids busy, or were they engaged in literacy tasks that will make a difference in their literate lives?" We pulled ourselves to our feet, heading over to the dreaded pile of children's work staring us in the face. Along the way we were distracted by the disarray of two of the centers we had worked so hard to create the previous weekend. We stopped to tidy and restock them with the materials needed for the next day, already dreading the next weekend when we would need to spend so much time creating more centers for the kids to help keep them busy.

Much later, when we were finished going through the pile of "things," we glanced at the clock. We realized that our fatigue was growing and that we had not even begun to look at the children's assessments from the last week or the focus lesson for writer's workshop the next day. We had spent the majority of our time preparing for and reviewing the children's busywork. Our kids didn't seem to be making the growth we believed they were capable of in literacy. We spent too much time managing their behavior, planning activities, and putting out fires instead of teaching. We didn't have time to plan for excellent instruction that would meet our children's needs, nor did we have enough time for small groups or individual conferences. We knew there had to be a better way.

Enter our classrooms a few years later. There is a quiet and calm hum to the room. Some children are lying on the floor with book boxes full of "good-fit" books sitting next to them. As they read to themselves, a child nearby reads the pictures in a book, giggling at a funny part. Another student takes notes from an interesting section on snow leopards in a *Zoobooks* magazine. One boy is singing along as he points to the words in his copy of our class songbook. Some children are curled up in a corner on pillows with partners, reading a particularly animated section from a Junie B. Jones book. Two others are taking turns as they choral-read a poem from *Take Me Out of the Bathtub: Poems for Two Voices*. Other students are scattered about at tables, heads bent, pens moving methodically across the pages of their journals, crafting tantalizing tall tales, silly songs, or a tearful retelling of a pet goldfish succumbing to old age at home last night. Near the word wall, others are sitting on the floor or at a table, tongues between their lips as they focus intently on building some of the word families and sight words using Wikki Stix, or writing some of their personal spelling words with play dough. Over on a couch, two students are wearing headphones, books in laps, as they listen to tapes of the books, turning the pages and following along with the voice on tape.

As you stand and look around, one thing seems to be missing: Where are the teachers? There we are, sitting on the floor with a group of four students. We are having an animated discussion about our favorite strategies to help us comprehend the story in front of us. We actually have our backs to the rest of the class. We're not even looking at them! Yet the rest of the children in the class are working by themselves, completely independent. Our intuitive sense of who needs to be redirected with a look or a verbal reminder goes unused as we focus our attention on the small group. We are not distracted by someone approaching us with a question or to tattle on another student, because it rarely happens. The rest of the class, away from our small, focused group, continues working independently.

As children leave for the day, we chat briefly with each one, mentioning something wonderful we saw them accomplish that day. We easily remember some happy moment, success, or exquisite thought each child had during the busy day and share it with them, bringing a smile to each face with promises of "We'll miss you until you return tomorrow!"

As we turn from the door, we quickly make a tour of the room, picking up a marker here, finding the lid to a wayward glue stick there. We stop at the computer to check our e-mail, return a phone call to a parent about next week's field trip, and make sure the chart rack has enough paper on it for the next day.

We then sit down to review today's assessments done with two children. We notice that Allie has made progress with the strategy "Back Up and Reread," and has developed some metacognitive awareness of its use. We write that observation down in our anecdotal notes and plan to reinforce this strategy with Allie the next time we meet with her. We take note of our running record with Devon. He still seems to have trouble with noticing the ends of words. We decide to pull him along with three other children who are having the same challenge, and work with them for the next few days on that skill. We review our notes on the progress of a guided group of five children who are all reading different books from the Magic Tree House series and working on their comprehension goals using the strategy of questioning. We make a note to double-check with Ingrid as she works diligently on the comprehension strategy called "Check for Understanding."

About thirty-five minutes have passed since the children have left the room. We look up from our work to check the time, glance toward the window, and notice the beautiful day outside. We scan the room one more time to be certain all is ready for tomorrow, grab our coats and keys, and head quickly to the door—still with enough daylight and enough energy for a long walk with the dog.

WHAT CHANGED?

These are two different pictures of our lives as literacy teachers. The latter is the one you will continue to see today. (Okay, so maybe it is not always sunny in Seattle. It is actually very rarely sunny here, so when the sun does shine, we have to get out there and enjoy it!)

The difference is our integration of the common core routines and framework we've come to call the Daily Five. When building this learning structure in our classrooms, it was critical to demonstrate and focus our teaching on what the child and teacher are to do inside each component. It is this explicit teaching and practicing of behaviors that sets the Daily Five apart from the other management systems we have tried over the years.

We never expected to create a new framework for our literacy block. We were frustrated with our inability to engage students in independent, meaningful reading practice. We just wanted someone to tell us what worked, and as the answer eluded us, we were forced to dig deeper. We called upon some of our favorite colleagues—Margaret Mooney, Regie Routman, Richard Allington, Lucy Calkins, Nancie Atwell, Steven Krashen, Michael Pressley, Irene Fountas and Gay Su Pinnell, and Shelley Harwayne, to name a few. We studied and read everything each of these people had published; we talked to each other daily about our discoveries. We were like Scott, a first grader in our class who was obsessed with trains. He read everything there was about trains; every story he wrote was about trains, and he played with trains every other second of the day. We too were obsessed, and determined to find a more effective way to help children be independent with meaningful activities, allowing us to work uninterrupted with small groups and individuals. We agreed with Gaea Leinhardt, Naomi Zigmond and William Cooley (1981), who found that the way teachers structure the learning environment and the way students spend their time influences the level of reading proficiency the students have attained at the end of the academic year.

Figure 1-1 Management: How We Have Evolved

Management Element	Our First Years of Teaching	Five Years Ago	Now with the Daily Five
Teaching and learning new behaviors	We would mention behaviors once and expect students to know and do them.	We would teach and practice behaviors once or twice and expect students to know and do them.	We teach and practice skills until behaviors become habits and "default" behaviors.
Expectations about the students	We thought students should come to us knowing the appropriate behaviors.	We thought most of the students should know these behaviors If not we would spend 1 or 2 lessons teaching them.	We know each class is different, and we spend at least 20 days building community, defining and practicing behaviors, building stamina, and assessing the needs of this particular group of children.

Figure 1-1 Management: How We Have Evolved *(continued)*

Management Element	Our First Years of Teaching	Five Years Ago	Now with the Daily Five
Monitoring student behaviors	We monitored students' behaviors.	We began releasing some student behaviors.	Students self-monitor their behaviors.
Whole group	Class points awarded for desired behaviors by teacher	Praised children for behaviors we expected them to exhibit; one student designated to record points awarded to class	Whole class practices, defines, and knows how to perform desired behaviors.
Small groups	Table points written on board and awarded by teacher	One child was table leader and recorded points awarded by teacher on chart at table for their group.	Groups of students practice and encourage each other on defined, desired behaviors.
Individual	Individual "star cards" with stars awarded by teacher	Individual recorded points when teacher said they had earned them.	Individual students reflect with self and confer with teacher and class about their particular behavior goals they are working to achieve.
Individual student not exhibiting desired behavior	Individuals "flip a card" from green to yellow to red enforced by teacher and displayed for whole class to view	Teacher gave a check mark or made note on her clipboard that only she saw. At three marks children stayed in for recess.	Individual may model correct behaviors for class.
	Individual stayed in for recess with head down.	Individual stayed in for recess and sat quietly.	Student may practice desired behavior for a short amount of time at recess. This desired behavior may become an articulated goal this child chooses to work on

Figure 1-1 Management: How We Have Evolved (continued)

Management Element	Our First Years of Teaching	Five Years Ago	Now with the Daily Five
Locus of control	Students had external locus of control. Teacher gave candy/treats for behaviors children were expected to exhibit.		Student have internal locus of control. Students have a sense of urgency with their time, learning, and behavior at school and hold each other responsible by encouraging and supporting each other.
Whose classroom is it?	It was "my classroom" until the end of the day, when we expected everyone to help clean it. Our teacher desk area took up one-fourth of the classroom.	Jobs were posted and "given" to students on a rotating basis. Our teacher desk area was getting smaller.	Students help make decisions about how to keep the room clean, create a plan for all to help, including the teacher. Our desk area takes up one-twenty-fourth of the classroom, as much as every other person occupying the room.
Where are supplies stored?	The stapler and tape were on our desk for our use. If the children needed to use these materials, we did it for them.	The stapler and tape were on the teacher desk. The children asked us to use them if they needed them.	Staplers and supplies are set out in a common area for all to use when they need them.

We began to look more closely at how we were structuring the learning environment, developing a new plan for how students would spend their time working independently while we met with small groups or conferred with individual students.

We wanted to change the atmosphere in our classrooms and our own roles, from trying to "manage" students, rushing around the room putting out fires, to creating routines and procedures that fostered independent literacy behaviors that were ingrained to the point of being habits. Our goal was for all students to have internalized these expectations and shared experiences in a way that allowed for every child to become engrossed in their reading and writing. We were no longer satisfied with drawing a clear line between our literacy curriculum and our management routines. Instead, we needed to work within our classroom communities to create environments where reading, writing, and self-monitoring were closely tied together for each child. We had to trust that our students had the skills and desire, even at age five, to accept the challenge of making thoughtful choices during sustained independent work periods.

With our focus more clearly defined, our attention shifted to what the experts had to say about students being independent and the tasks that facilitated their independent learning.

THE DAILY FIVE EVOLVE

Our first encounter with the Daily Five came when we were studying with Margaret Mooney, a literacy instructional expert from New Zealand. While she was explicitly modeling a guided reading lesson to a group of teachers, someone stopped the whole group and frantically said, "Margaret, I can't see how guided reading would work in my class. You see, I have thirty students. What are the rest of my kids doing while I'm trying to teach this small group of children?"

"Oh, you know," Margaret said. "They're reading, reading to each other, revisiting books, writing, and trying something new."

We quickly wrote these down, and remember saying, "That seems too simple. What about centers, what about worksheets? How will we ever know students are learning if they don't hand in pages for us to correct? How can you ever get all of your students to do all those tasks independently?"

We consulted our colleagues' work again to see if they agreed with Margaret about these tasks. Was this really what we could have our students doing while we worked with small groups or individuals? What did the research say about each task?

As we persevered, we found what many researchers already knew and had been saying for years. These were the tasks that made a difference in classrooms where students were achieving.

The list we first heard from Margaret evolved into the following five tasks, which continually surfaced in our investigation: read to yourself, read to someone, work on writing, listen to reading, and spelling/word study. (See Figure 1-2 for the research base that supports these five activities.) These tasks were a much longer reading block than we had ever had, yet we still had to find a way to help the children work independently to complete them. Easier said than done! Allington (2001) suggests that children should spend a minimum of one and a half hours a day reading in school. Instructional time is in addition to these ninety minutes.

Figure 1-2 The Daily Five Research Base

Read to Yourself

The best way to become a better reader is to practice each day, with books you choose, on your just-right reading level. It soon becomes a habit.

Allington, R. and P. Johnston. 2002. *Reading to Learn: Lessons From Exemplary Fourth-Grade Classrooms.* New York: Guilford Press.

Morrow, L., L. Gambrell, and M. Pressley. 2003. *Best Practices in Literacy Instruction.* New York: Guilford Press.

Marshall, J. C. 2000. *Are They Really Reading?* Portland, ME: Stenhouse Publishers.

Krashen, S. 2004. *The Power of Reading: Insights from the Research.* Portsmouth, NH: Heinemann.

Pressley, M., R. Allington, R. Wharton-McDonald, C. Block, and L. Morrow. 2001. *Learning to Read: Lessons from Exemplary First-Grade Classrooms.* New York: Guilford Press.

Routman, R. 2003. *Reading Essentials: The Specifics You Need to Teach Reading Well.* Portsmouth, NH: Heinemann.

Read to Someone

Reading to someone allows for more time to practice strategies, helping you work on fluency and expression, check for understanding, hear your own voice, and share in the learning community.

Allington, R. 2001. *What Really Matters for Struggling Readers: Designing Research-Based Programs.* New York: Addison-Wesley Longman.

Miller, D. 2002. *Reading with Meaning: Teaching Comprehension in the Primary Grades.* Portland, ME: Stenhouse Publishers.

Work on Writing

Just like reading, the best way to become a better writer is to practice writing each day.

Fletcher, R. and J. Portalupi. 2002. *Craft Lessons: Teaching Writing K–8.* Portland, ME: Stenhouse Publishers.

Graves, D. 1985. "All Children Can Write." *Learning Disablilities Focus* 1(1), 36–43.

Routman, R. 2005. *Writing Essentials.* Portsmouth, NH: Heinemann.

Listen to Reading

We hear examples of good literature and fluent reading. We learn more words, thus expanding our vocabulary and becoming better readers.

Allen, J. 2001. *Yellow Brick Roads: Shared and Guided Paths to Independent Reading 4–12.* Portland, ME: Stenhouse Publishers.

Trelease, J. 2001. *The Read-Aloud Handbook.* New York: Penguin Books.

Figure 1-2 The Daily Five Research Base *(continued)*

Spelling/Word Work

Correct spelling allows for more fluent writing, thus speeding up the ability to write and get thinking down on paper. This is an essential foundation for writers.

Marten, C. 2003. *Word Crafting: Teaching Spelling, Grades K–6*. Portsmouth, NH: Heinemann.

Snowball, D. and F. Bolton. 1999. *Spelling K–8: Planning and Teaching*. Portland, ME: Stenhouse Publishers.

Gentry, R. J. 2004. *The Science of Spelling: The Explicit Specifics that Make Great Readers and Writers (and Spellers!)* Portsmouth, NH: Heinemann.

WHAT SETS THE DAILY FIVE APART?

Think about how you manage your literacy block right now. Are you using a basal, seatwork, centers, reader's/writer's workshops, or a combination of these? We have found ourselves using all four at one time or another. Looking back at our teaching experiences, we have noticed a definite progression in the way we have managed our literacy block. We began with a teacher-driven model that relied on busywork and artificial reading and writing activities (worksheets and so on). We slowly progressed through centers to where we are now, with the Daily Five. The Daily Five is a student-driven management structure designed to fully engage students in reading and writing.

Figure 1-3 Our Literacy Block Development Over Time

Teacher Driven	Student Driven
Low student engagement	High student engagement
Tended to be busywork activities	Meaningful reading and writing
Artificial reading and writing	Authentic reading and writing
Little time spent reading	Majority of time spent reading

Seatwork Basal Program	Centers	Workshop	Daily Five

Most of us are familiar with basals, seatwork, and centers. They are structures many of us learned during our teacher preparation programs. Many teachers have since ventured into reader's and writer's workshops, which have some similarities to the Daily Five. These commonalities may lead teachers to think that the workshop model is the same as the Daily Five. What distinguishes the Daily Five from other management models is that the Daily Five:

- Rely on the teaching of independence
- Manage the entire literacy block
- Allow for three to five focus lessons and more intentional teaching
- Provide students substantial time to read and write
- Allow for the integration of reading and writing
- Incorporate a variety of clearly defined instructional routines that accelerate learning
- Build stamina to ensure longer periods of time students successfully read and write
- Articulate student behaviors that culminate in highly engaged learners
- Teach students to understand and monitor their literacy goals

HOLDING THE LITERACY BLOCK TOGETHER

The first weeks of school for any teacher are about setting the daily structure and building community. If you had asked us years ago what curriculum we tackled in the first six weeks of school, we would have replied that we didn't "do" curriculum during this early stretch—the time was all about understanding expectations and learning how to be respectful of peers.

Now we approach the first weeks of school differently. The Daily Five is the largest part of our literacy curriculum each day—it is the structure that allows all children to do meaningful work independently as we work in small groups and with individual children. The first weeks of school are dedicated to launching the Daily Five and instilling literacy habits that allow for independent work with little or no teacher supervision.

This book is about how to launch the Daily Five, regardless of what time of year you are reading this. If you are frustrated because you are spending too much time trying to manage students, and not enough time offering the most rigorous and joyful literacy curriculum possible, then the structure of the Daily Five may be what you are looking for.

As professionals, we are asked to include an inordinate amount in our literacy programs. We are expected to teach specific reading strategies to increase comprehension, accuracy, fluency, and vocabulary. Reading needs to be addressed through shared and guided reading, and partner and independent reading, as well as read-aloud. We must provide opportunities for children to write, and we need to teach both form and process. We are expected to teach student behaviors of independence and self-monitoring, and we need to motivate children. Through it all, we are expected to assess our students both informally and formally and then

Figure 1-4 The Daily Five Literacy Block

During each of the independent work periods, students are cycling through their choice of one of the Daily Five components. We have four thirty-minute independent work periods daily; the fifth is optional if time permits.

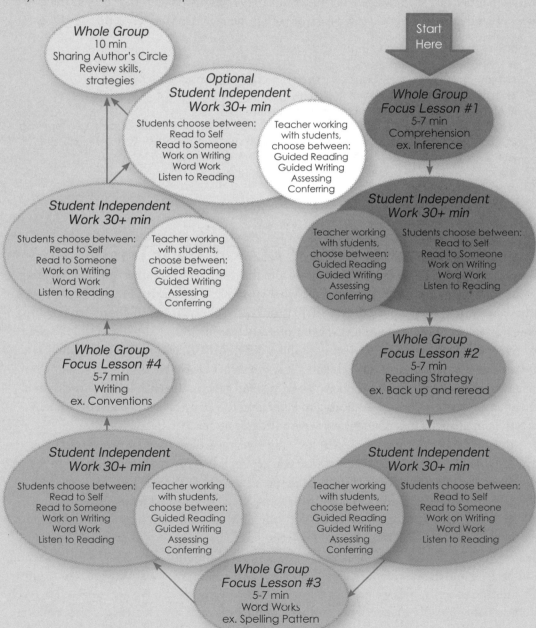

differentiate their instruction. How can we possibly do all of these things without losing important pieces, or for that matter, losing our minds? The Daily Five is a structure that envelops all of the components of comprehensive literacy and provides us with a plan to manage each piece in a user friendly way.

This book does not present our entire literacy curriculum—it is about helping students develop independent literacy habits, so that we are free to work with small groups or have individual conferences. Once the Daily Five has become a habit for students, we use instructional time to present daily focus lessons on comprehension strategies, writer's craft, phonics, and other components of our literacy curriculum to the whole class. Our Daily Five literacy block looks something like Figure 1.4 by mid-October, after students have learned how to work independently. As we work in small groups or confer with or assess individual students, children cycle through Daily Five activities of their choice in the two-hour session. They are responsible for ensuring they have accomplished a different component of the Daily Five in each half-hour work period.

This book is not a prescription for literacy success. It is about developing shared awareness and instructional routines with students, through specific, focused teaching, while balancing students' needs for choice and independence. Join us as we further explore the Daily Five, a structure that supports learning in any classroom and leads to children who are self-winding lifelong readers.

02

FROM "MANAGEMENT" TO "PRINCIPLED HABITS": FOUNDATIONS OF THE DAILY FIVE

■■■□□

It is not enough to be busy, so are the ants. The question is: What are we busy about?

—Henry David Thoreau

■■■□□

What beliefs influence the decisions you make in your classroom? Are there foundational principles you cling to that support your teaching strategies and learning for all students? As we begin to share what is important and essential to the Daily Five, the following core foundations emerge:

- trusting students
- providing choice
- nurturing community
- creating a sense of urgency
- building stamina
- staying out of students' way once routines are established

TRUST

We believe positive relationships are the first and most vital element of our children's learning process. Meaningful learning requires respect between the teacher and students as well as among the students themselves. We treat children as valuable individuals, each one unique and worthy of respect and caring. We continually remind ourselves that in the face of the public push for higher test scores, we must not let ourselves or our students get caught up in a frenzied pace. Taking time to build trust and demonstrate caring is the foundation upon which all other elements of our literacy learning are built.

Many of us have experienced living with a new driver in our homes. Remember when your teenager sat next to you, but behind the wheel for the first time? That critical moment occurred after you'd taught him or her enough skills to be successful on his or her first outing. You trusted your child, and your child had the confidence in his or her newly acquired skills to take that fledgling outing. There was an unspoken understanding that if your child encountered trouble, he or she would not be left without support to successfully navigate the way. As William Bridges says in *Managing Transitions*, "Without trust in the teacher, the step toward independence and the mastery of a new skill is less likely to happen. At that moment, with fear balanced against hope, it is trust that makes the difference" (p. 108).

Trusting children is the underpinning of what makes the Daily Five (or any structure for teaching children to manage themselves independently) work. When trust is combined with explicit instruction, our students acquire the skills necessary to become independent learners. Students will continue their learning even when they are not being "managed" by the teacher, thus shifting the management of behavior from the teacher to the individual students.

One day we told our students we would not be in school the next day because we were attending a teaching conference. Mick promptly spoke up, saying there would be no need to have a guest teacher (substitute) while we were out because "Those guest teachers just bug us and won't leave us alone to read and write." We often observe in wonder and amazement how engaged they are during Daily Five, functioning independently without our interference.

When students execute the skills of independence they have been taught, teachers are free to focus their time and energy on instruction. This instruction takes various forms, as teachers are free to pull one or more students aside, tailoring groups or conferences to meet specific needs of each child. It is not unusual for an adult to walk into the class, bend over, and ask one of the children where their teacher is. Quite often, the child has no idea. They are so independent and engaged in what they are doing that we can easily work with small groups and individuals without interrupting their work.

In *Reading with Meaning,* Debbie Miller says, "What am I doing now that I could trust the kids to do?" and "In what ways could I trust children where I haven't before? Think about things like: Do they really need to go to the bathroom and get a drink all at the same time? . . . Do I need to count and monitor the number of pretzels or animal crackers they take for snack, or can they be trusted to take two or three? . . . Do I really need elaborate and time-consuming check-out systems for books, CDs? . . . I say no, not when we're clear about what we expect and why. Not when we trust kids enough to show them how" (p. 22). These are questions we continue to ask ourselves as well.

Without the belief that children can be trusted, we had a difficult time with the whole idea of Daily Five. We would underestimate our students' abilities because we thought kids could not read or write that long on their own. The Daily Five works because we trust our students, but it is not a blind trust. Through lessons and guided practice, we gradually build behaviors that can be sustained over time so children can easily be trusted to manage on their own.

CHOICE

Children love structure and routine. Each year we put daily schedules on our boards. After reviewing the daily schedule in the morning, children take ownership, refer to it, and keep us on-task. "Teacher, it's ten thirty—time for recess." There is comfort and safety in the reliability of the routine. Children love the structure and routine of the Daily Five as well. However, there are a couple of differences for children and the teacher compared with a typical school day. The most pronounced difference for students is the choice they have over the order in which they'll participate in the Daily Five activities. During the literacy block, five tasks are taking place simultaneously:

- Reading to Self
- Reading to Someone
- Listening to Reading
- Working on Writing
- Spelling/Word Work

The order students choose varies from day to day, depending on their goals, motivation, and mood.

When we first gave children the power to choose, we were a little nervous. We were used to owning the clock, the schedule, and even their learning, an operating mode supported by messages from administrators such as, "Here's your basal series—teach it" or, "This is your curriculum for this year—get through it all by June 20." It wasn't meeting the needs of every child, and in our hearts we knew it wasn't right for us, so we developed an alternative approach.

We began by asking ourselves, "What meaningful activities does research say my students should be engaging in that puts them in charge of their own learning, is self-motivating, is worthy of their time and effort, and will improve their skills?" Students plan their days in our classrooms with a few important questions in mind:

- What are my goals in reading and writing?
- What will I do first?
- Whom will I work with?
- What will I accomplish?
- What was I working on yesterday that I want to continue today?

With the introduction of choice a child's world changes. Morrow, Gambrell, and Pressley (2003) say in their book *Best Practices in Literacy Instruction,*

We would like to see more student choice in reading lessons and greater encouragement of students to read a great deal, including many more communications to students that reading provides great pleasure, and that choosing to read is choosing to do something that is fun. We would also like to see more emphasis on students' choosing to be strategic, to be impressed more with the message than to be in charge of their reading and the processes they use during reading, that is, with the idea that they are to become self-regulated readers. Perhaps if that emphasis on self-regulation were heightened, there would be more automatic transfer of mental comprehension processes to novel texts. (p. 120)

Choice is highly motivational and puts children in charge of their learning. Camille, a sixth-grade teacher, implemented choice in her reading workshop and said she will never go back.

My children have never been so engaged in their own learning, and so motivated to read and write. It has usually been a struggle getting the reluctant readers to choose books to read on their own, and then they rarely read. Now, with choice, these children spend time telling me that I must read the story they are reading. We can now have conversations about what they have read rather than about whether they have read the books I chose for them or not.

We know a principal whose superintendent gave him three books to read over the summer. Two were chosen for him and one was the principal's choice (although the choice did need to be within the genre of the superintendent's choice). Needless to say, the book that represented some choice for the principal was much easier and more enjoyable to read than the other two. When you have some say in the matter, you are much more motivated to complete the task.

We have often encountered kids who appear to be unmotivated. At times they are battling for some kind of control in their lives, so we give it to them through the vehicle of choice.

Purpose + Choice = Motivation. It is not unusual to overhear children say, "Want to do Read to Someone first today? I just got a great book at the library!" or "Can I have the Kevin Henkes book you were reading during Daily Five yesterday? I want to read it today." Marilyn said one morning, "I can't WAIT to do Work on Writing today. I lost my tooth and the Tooth Fairy came. I want to write about what she left me!" We didn't see that kind of excitement and enthusiasm when we told students what they had to read and what they had to write.

COMMUNITY

We spend a great deal of effort creating and maintaining a healthy classroom culture. What the class experiences together weaves the tapestry that will create an environment of learning and caring for all students. Each new group of children will fashion their own unique community based on the schema they bring to the classroom and the experiences they have during that year.

Creating a community starts with getting to know each other the first day of school and is embedded in the schedules we design together, the rules we construct together, and the stories we read and draw on. The tapestry of the community becomes more intricate with each shared activity and lesson. For example, after concluding a Kevin Henkes author study with *Lilly's Purple Plastic Purse,* it wasn't unusual to hear someone say for weeks afterward, "Wow. That is about all I can say: Wow." Our shared experiences and knowledge bind us together.

A sense of community provides members with ownership to hold others accountable for behaviors of effort, learning, order, and kindness. When Michelle had a difficult time staying focused on her book, Talon quietly and respectfully redirected her, referring to the I-chart, a brainstormed list of behaviors for Read to Self.

During the Daily Five, students may come one step closer to achieving goals they have set for themselves. The whole community knows and rejoices in their progress. If a student is disrupting others during their work time, the community will join together to encourage, support, and hold this child accountable for his or her learning behavior. It is group dynamics at its finest. The "how-to's" for building community are an integral part of each and every lesson.

SENSE OF URGENCY

We all have a deep need to know why we have to do something. Children and adults alike tend to recoil at answers such as, "Because you have to" or "Because it's our policy." Whether audibly or not we often find ourselves asking, "What's in it for me?" For that reason we always teach *why* we do things. Creating urgency in learning establishes a culture where every moment of learning and practicing counts for students and teachers. It is not anxiety that teachers and students feel when they are teaching and learning with a sense of urgency, but a responsibility to take ownership for their own teaching and learning. Regie Routman (2003) speaks of teaching with this sense of urgency to provide the highest-quality instruction for our students.

We believe that when people understand the reason for a task, it establishes motivation and becomes a force that keeps them persevering. As we think about teaching each one of the Daily Five, we start with explicitly explaining *why*

- you read to yourselves;
- you read to someone;
- you listen to reading;
- you write;
- you do word work.

For each Daily Five choice the sense of urgency comes from understanding the *why*. The purpose for each task is clear, so the activity becomes worthy of concentrated effort and time. When we begin each lesson by telling our children why we are taking time to teach the idea or concept, we consistently see more motivation and on-task behavior no matter what we are teaching.

Children need to know that researchers say reading each day is the best way to become a better reader and that the best readers practice each day with books they choose. When done enough, reading will soon become an enjoyable habit.

We'll never forget the time we had two tall vice principals observing the Daily Five in action. We were sitting on the floor with a small group of children. The rest of the class was scattered about the room independently working on their Daily Five choices. The room had the lovely hum that comes from children who are comfortable, happy, and actively engaged in what they are doing. The vice principals discussed their observations, and their deep voices resonated above the hum. Jenna, a fairly quiet child who uses her words sparingly, walked up to the men, tugged the pant leg of one, and said in no uncertain terms, "Mister, can you take it outside? I am working on Read to Self. I really need to practice to be a better reader. My brain is busy and your loud voice is stopping it. How am I ever going to be better if you are so noisy?"

He glanced at us with a bemused expression on his face, held his hands up in front of him as if to say, "I give!" and backed quietly out of the room. Jenna walked back to the corner of the couch she had previously occupied and went back to reading.

Jenna had a sense of urgency, the kind we want to instill in every child—the feeling that reading is so important that they can't and won't let anything get in their way.

STAMINA

The stamina needed for the Daily Five is much like the stamina needed for physical exercise. A month after I (Gail) had my second daughter, I was determined to get back into shape. I decided to join a health club and have a trainer help familiarize me with the equipment and get me started. I entered the first day with high hopes, and a helpful (fifteen years my junior) instructor started me off on the stationary bike. "This will be easy," he remarked while setting the timer for twenty minutes. "When you finish, I'll get you going on the treadmill." After ten minutes, I was feeling fatigued and worn out. I had no stamina or muscle memory to rely on. I didn't want to seem like a wimp, so I buoyed myself with self-talk such as, "I used to be an athlete. . . . I can do this. . . . I'm just a little out of shape." But after fifteen minutes I was feeling nauseous and every muscle was in revolt. I stopped, staggered to the locker room, changed my clothes, and sneaked out, never to return to that gym again.

We think about reading the same way. If we start with a task that children have no stamina for or lack the ability to do, they are not only doomed to frustration and failure, but why would they ever return to that activity on their own? When children begin anything of importance, they deserve to have a teacher who will lay the foundation for success, support them, cheer them on, and help them succeed. Had I been supported and given manageable tasks that gradually increased in time and resistance, it wouldn't have taken me ten years to return to a gym. Our children need our support from the minute they walk into our classrooms.

Building stamina works with even our youngest students. Dan is a five-year-old boy in our class. His extremely tired dad had been working nights and hadn't had much sleep for weeks. He came into our class the other day and said, "I curse you and the day you taught my son the word *stamina.* I was tucking Dan in the other night and having a hard time staying awake through the end of our bedtime story. Suddenly, Dan piped up and said, 'Gee, Dad, we've gotta work on your stamina.'" The poor man had bags under his eyes and was asking us, "Couldn't you just teach him to finger-paint or something?" The power of building stamina is enormous.

It's like an analogy of the child who plays soccer. We drive up to the field and roll down the window and ask the coach, "When will practice be over? When should I be back to pick her up?" If the coach were to reply, "In seven minutes," we would question the quality of the soccer program. Who can get better at soccer practicing only seven minutes a day? The same idea applies to reading and writing.

Just like with soccer practice, children cannot become better readers, make standards, and develop a love for reading when we are giving them only seven minutes a day to do it. If we are instructing so much that the students don't get a chance to read, or if we are counting working in a workbook as reading time, then we're not giving them enough time to become better readers and writers.

The Daily Five allows for teachers to have instruction time in one-on-one and small-group settings because the bulk of the class is independently engaged in worthwhile and meaningful activities. This independent work time is the time for children to be practicing their reading strategies. In the beginning we found that our children could do each of the components of the Daily Five, just not for extended periods of time. That's why we started looking at how we teach children to read to themselves and realized the need to help them build stamina.

We couldn't spend all our time and energy keeping kids on-task, because if we did, there would not be enough time to teach, children would not have enough practice time, and therefore they would never make the progress they needed to meet standards. As teachers we needed them to be independent so we could use that time to individualize instruction for every student.

We needed to teach children how to build their stamina for independent work. We had the opportunity to introduce this in a kindergarten classroom. The students were able to read silently for only one minute on the first day. After focused instruction and only one week's practice, they had increased their on-task independent reading time to ten minutes. The day we did not go in, children went up to their teacher and said, "Ms. Pak, we didn't do our reading. How can we get better at stamina if we don't read?" After building slowly, a minute at a time, they were having success and were motivated to continue.

Teaching children how to read on their own for extended periods of time each day creates the self-winding learner that we want in the center of our comprehensive literacy program. Students are actively engaged in the reading process when they have the stamina to read on their own.

STAY OUT OF THE WAY

Once children understand what is expected of them, have practiced strategies, and have built their stamina, it is time for us to put into place our next belief principle—which is to stay out of the way and let them read. This may sound counterintuitive, but we want students to make decisions on their own and to monitor themselves regarding their progress. How can they possibly do that if never given the chance to try it on their own in a safe, caring environment such as our classrooms?

Many years ago, when we were developing the Daily Five, we had an interesting experience. We didn't stay out of the children's way as they were practicing. We did what we thought all good elementary teachers did. As the children were practicing Read to Self and building their stamina, we went around the room to each child, quietly telling them what a wonderful job they were doing as readers. We were proud of their ability to stay focused, and believed that we needed to constantly reinforce their on-task behavior.

The first day students read without our hovering reinforcement, their behavior fell apart. They were up and walking around, bothering others, going to the bathroom, getting drinks, chatting with their friends, and coming to us asking what they should do. We realized they had anchored their behavior to our reactions. We had unwittingly taught them to rely on our reinforcement to keep them on-task. They were not the least bit independent.

This was a difficult but empowering lesson to learn. It is a mistake we have tried not to repeat and one we are careful to address when talking to teachers about the Daily Five. Now we'll dig a little deeper into the lessons, materials, and procedures we use to help our students develop this independence.

03

WHAT'S THE DIFFERENCE?: KEY MATERIALS, CONCEPTS, AND ROUTINES FOR LAUNCHING THE DAILY FIVE

■ ■ ■ ■ ■

When we follow routines day after day, our students can use their energy to grow as readers and learners rather than to figure out what we expect them to do. And we in turn, can focus our energy on teaching, not managing, our independent learners.

—Kathy Collins

■ ■ ■ ■ ■

Although the foundations of the Daily Five create a strong base for student independence, there are also key materials, routines, and concepts we introduce to children in the first days of school that are crucial to the success of the program:

- ■ Establishing a gathering place for brain and body breaks
- ■ Developing the concept of "good-fit" books through a series of lessons
- ■ Creating anchor charts with students for referencing behaviors
- ■ Short, repeated intervals of independent practice
- ■ Calm signals and check-in procedures
- ■ Using the correct model/incorrect model approach for demonstrating appropriate behaviors

We will explain each of these components separately.

ESTABLISHING A GATHERING PLACE

Gathering kids in front for instruction, releasing them to practice, and then bringing them back to share their thinking represents the steady flow that is at the heart of effective teaching and learning. (p. 31)

—*Stephanie Harvey and Anne Goudvis, **Strategies That Work: Teaching Comprehension to Enhance Understanding***

A gathering place is an open space large enough for the whole class to come together and sit on the floor. The space also includes a chart rack and whiteboard for focus lessons, the anchor charts created by the class, poem and song charts, an overhead projector, and other teaching materials.

Regardless of the age of children we teach, we always have a gathering place. We used to think that once children move into intermediate grades they are too big to gather together on the floor. We have found this not to be true. A gathering place is yet another way to influence children to be successful. By having the whole class sitting right in front of us, distractions are limited and proximity allows us to check in on behavior more effectively. Another benefit is that students are able to turn and talk to each other, engaging everyone in the conversation of a lesson.

During the Daily Five we bring the whole class together at the gathering place after each work session. As children join us in the gathering place on the floor, it signals a shift in activity and thinking.

This shift accomplishes two things: it provides time for a change in their brain work along with much-needed movement of their bodies. We call this a Brain and Body Break.

GOOD-FIT BOOKS

At the Illinois State Reading Council Conference in March 2005, Richard Allington stated that the most current research indicates that an independent-level or good-fit book for children is one they can read with 99 percent accuracy. This is a shift from the 1946 research by Betts, who concluded that a good-fit-level book was one that children could read with 95 percent or greater accuracy.

Gambrell, Wilson and Gantt (1981) said higher levels of oral reading error rate were linked to significant increases in off-task behavior. Given what the current research and leaders in our field are saying, we find it is essential to spend focused classroom time teaching our children to choose books that are a good fit for them, books they enjoy and that, as Routman (2004) says, "seem custom-made for the child" (p. 93).

Figure 3-1 Focus Lesson on Reading Pictures at the Gathering Place

An abundance of material has been written on the topic of choosing good-fit books. Fountas and Pinnell's *Guiding Readers and Writers Grades 3–6* (2001) along with *Still Learning to Read* by Sibberson and Szymusiak (2003) have whole sections devoted to the topic of helping children choose appropriate books. As classroom teachers, we understand how important the role of good-fit books is in the classroom, but believe the real challenge lies with our teaching children so they are empowered to choose good-fit books for themselves each time they go to the library, bookstore, or classroom book area.

As we worked with our children over the years to find this simple strategy, it became clear that there was more to choosing a good-fit book than simply reading most of the words correctly. We began to understand that a child's purpose for reading, interest in a topic, and ability to comprehend played as large a role in finding a good-fit book as readability did. Thus, the birth of the "I PICK" good-fit books lesson.

Nearly daily throughout the school year we have conversations about good-fit books. It's a simple message with great implications that require frequent conversations to help children learn. We teach children that one of the most important things to do to become a better reader is to read good-fit books. We look for a good-fit book in five ways using the acronym I PICK.

Figure 3-2 I PICK Good-Fit Books

I PICK

1. **I** choose a book
2. **P** urpose—Why do I want to read it?
3. **I** nterest—Does it interest me?
4. **C** omprehend—Am I understanding what I am reading?
5. **K** now—I know most of the words

We teach children about choosing good-fit books by comparing book selection to shoe selection. Our opening lesson on finding good-fit books is an anchor lesson that we refer to all year long. We come to school with a bag of shoes. Inside our bag we have placed a pair of our "Sunday best" shoes, tennis shoes, snow boots, golf shoes, and our husband's much-too-large shoes. We begin by pulling out each pair of shoes one at a time and asking our class what they think the purpose of these shoes is.

As we pull out the shoes, we talk about them: "Each pair of shoes has its purpose. I certainly would not wear snow boots to play golf! Just like choosing which shoes to wear for which activity, we also have a purpose when

Figure 3-3 Shoe Lesson for I PICK Good-Fit Books

we choose a book. The purpose for choosing a book may be because you want to learn about a certain topic or just to read for fun."

During the examination of the shoes the discussion moves to interest. We guide our students to see that we do not have soccer shoes in our bag because we are not interested in playing soccer. However, we love to golf, play in the snow, and as the well-worn tennis shoes convey, go for long walks as well. Conversations evolve into what shoes we would wear for our Interest. We then discuss the importance of choosing books that interest us as well.

We share with them, "Just like the way our shoes reflect our interests, it is important we pick books that interest us." We share a variety of books we are interested in and ones we do not have much interest in. The class discussion turns to favorite genres, authors, and types of books that interest each student.

With the current emphasis in professional reading on helping kids choose good-fit books, we had too often overlooked children's interest in books. Nationwide there is extensive focus on lexile levels, readability levels, and so forth, and oftentimes we forget that children, like adults, need to be interested in what they are reading. This is especially true if we are to get them to read the volume of material that will help them move from being a "survival" reader to a lifelong reader who chooses to read for knowledge and pleasure.

Before teaching the last two steps of choosing a good-fit book, we go back to our bag of shoes. We pull out our husband's much-too-large shoes, put them on, and proceed to try to move around the room. Amid giggles and peals of laughter we point out that these shoes are too big, so they don't fit. This is just like a book that is either too hard to read or that we don't understand. The shoes don't fit and neither does the book.

We have now opened up the lines of communication for creating not only a classroom of children who are learning to choose good-fit books, but a room where all children are honored and respected for the types of books each needs to read to move toward the goal of being a better reader.

We then have a few students who clearly have different-size feet remove one shoe. We ask them to trade that one shoe with another student who has a shoe that might fit their purpose and interest. When the traded shoes don't fit, we can talk once again about the shoes meeting their needs of purpose and interest but not fitting. "This is just like books! Books that are a good fit for one student may not be a good fit for another." This also is the perfect time to talk about students who wear the correctly fitting shoe.

"If Emily has on her own gym shoes and is in the gym, she has a good-fit pair of shoes; they are a good-fit pair of shoes for her because they are the correct shoes for her purpose, her interest, and are not too big or too small—they fit. She can be very successful in gym wearing shoes that are a good fit. If she has a book that is a good fit for her, she will be very successful reading that book. Ben's gym shoes also are the correct shoes for Emily's purpose and interest, but they are way too big for her. She will not be successful in gym wearing those shoes because they are not a good fit. Likewise if she is reading Ben's book that may be too hard, it is not a good fit and she will not be successful, not to mention it is just not fun."

We explain that there are two more ways to know if a book is a good fit: comprehension—understand what you read, and know most of the words. This type of dialog is a yearlong anchor in our classroom to help children understand that we must pick books for our interest and purpose and ones that fit for us to be successful, just like we pick shoes. We all need to have books that fulfill our purpose and interest along with our being able to know the words and comprehend what they say.

We model the last two components of I PICK with books we have brought to school. We use a picture book, a good-fit chapter book, and a finance magazine, in which we can

Figure 3-4 Picking Good-Fit Books

read the words but can't explain what the articles mean, thus modeling a lack of comprehension. We usually check out a medical journal from the library to use as an example of not knowing the words. We go through each book, modeling our use of the I PICK method for each one.

After we complete the lesson for the day, we spend time helping kids find books using the new I PICK strategy. We may do that in our classroom, provided we have ample books to choose from, or we go into the school library, with our I PICK chart in tow for reference. We always meet with our librarian if she is going to be helping kids pick out books and ask her if she would be willing to lend a hand with this system. Using common language helps reinforce the skill.

When a child comes and asks for help finding a good-fit book, we go through the very same process each and every time. First we ask them what their **purpose** is. Is it to find a good story to read during the Daily Five, a book to help support a report they are doing, or a book to read just for fun?

Then we ask them what they are **interested** in. Do they want a book a bit like the one they just finished and loved so much? Do they devour mysteries and want more? Or perhaps they are interested in learning more about our pet rats and want information so they can write their own rat book. Only upon the completion of such a conversation can we move into helping and teaching kids how to locate books, and sample the text to see if the book fits the last two elements of a good-fit book for them—**comprehend**, and **know** the words. Teaching a child to check for comprehension takes extensive guided practice and oftentimes consistently checking their books with them each time we meet in a one-on-one conference or small guided group. Know the words is a bit simpler: if they know all the words, it is a good-fit book for them.

As children grasp the concept of I PICK, we have them model their book choices in front of the whole class. Seeing their peers choosing good-fit books over and over helps cement the idea for the rest of the class.

The week we do this lesson, we also send home a newsletter to families telling them about I PICK and asking for their help and support. We revisit I PICK in our newsletters at least once a month to keep it on the front burner for the kids as well as their caregivers.

Children who learn to select good-fit books will no longer wander aimlessly in a library or classroom collection looking for a book. They have tools that enable them to end up with a book that is a good fit for them. We know that the very best way to grow as a reader is to spend lots of time reading, and the majority of that time needs to be with a good-fit book.

For children to read independently and practice reading, they need a variety of books at their direct disposal. In our classrooms each child has a book box. (See Figure 3-4.) A book box can be a magazine box, a zippered plastic bag, a tub, or even a cereal box covered with Contact paper. Each child has his or her own book box filled with three to eight good-fit books.

Having a variety of good-fit books for all children is a vital piece to creating independence with children in the classroom. After all, hasn't every one of us experienced, at one time or another, the frustration of having students who spent the majority of their independent reading time looking for a book instead of reading? Not to mention the number of children they would take off-task with them as they were "shopping for a book"? Oftentimes, our most at-risk readers or those who feel unsuccessful are the most skilled at "shopping for books" instead of participating in the act that we know will help them the most: reading the whole time.

SETTING UP BOOK BOXES

At the beginning of each year, we often do not know our children's reading levels, favorite books, or favorite genres. However, to begin teaching the independent behaviors of the Daily Five, children must have a book box filled with books for this training period. Therefore, we spend a few minutes before the first day of school filling each child's book box with three to eight picture books, magazines, and easy chapter books. Children will use these books right away on Day One. After the good-fit lessons, children will begin to put their own selections into their book boxes.

Figure 3-5 Sample Selections for Book Boxes

Sample Book Box of Beginning Reader's (Level A-I) (Fountas and Pinnell's leveling system) Self-Selected Books Based on I PICK	Sample Book Box of Intermediate Reader's (Level I-P) Self-Selected Books Based on I PICK	Sample Book Box of Advanced Reader's (Level Q-Z) Self-Selected Books Based on I PICK
■ *Don't Let the Pigeon Drive the Bus* by Mo Willems ■ *No, David!* by David Shannon ■ *Look* by Tana Hoban ■ *Get Down Danny* by Mia Coulton ■ *Big Fat Hen* by Keith Baker ■ *Cat in the Hat* by Dr. Seuss	■ *Junie B. Jones Has a Peep in Her Pocket* by Barbara Park ■ *Magic Tree House: Civil War on Sunday* by Mary Pope Osborne ■ *Take Me Out of the Bathtub* by Alan Katz	■ *The Tale of Despereaux* by Kate DiCamillo ■ *This Side of Paradise* by Steven Layne ■ *Zoobooks* Magazine ■ *The Aliens Have Landed* by Kenn Nesbitt

We acquire books for children's book boxes in a variety of ways. We have become fixtures at our public and school libraries. Both libraries allow us to check out forty picture books at a time. They happily print out a copy of all the titles, which we use to help us when it comes time to return the books. We begin each year with a letter to our families asking them to keep us in mind when they are cleaning out bookshelves at home. We also ask families to keep their eyes open as they visit local thrift shops or garage sales. We let them know titles, authors, or series we are particularly interested in.

Figure 3-6 A portion of the classroom library is devoted to finding good-fit books.

Our ultimate goal has been to add to our classroom libraries each and every year. Jim Trelease (2001) says that children in classrooms with the most books consistently outperform their peers who are in classrooms with little or no library.

ANCHOR CHARTS

In her book *Reading with Meaning,* Debbie Miller describes anchor charts as large (24-by-36-inch) charts created based on what children have to say. These charts are one way to make thinking permanent and visible in the classroom. Anchor charts also allow the class members to trace their work together, build on earlier learning, or simply remember a specific lesson (2002, p. 56).

While observing classrooms in New Zealand, we were amazed by the practice of permanently displaying charts. If something is important, it is written down, and learning becomes anchored to these charts. This visible learning makes up the tapestry of the year and the decorations of the classroom. Hence all work is kept and constantly referred to. Disposing of it would be throwing away a connection to prior thinking and learning. Students can remember where they were sitting at the time the charts were created, thus constructing memories, schema, background knowledge, and background experiences that become the multidimensional layers each one uses to create meaning and understanding in his or her educational life.

Figure 3-7 Anchor Charts for Read to Self

As each component of the Daily Five is introduced, the class comes together to make an anchor chart, which we call an "I" (for independence) chart. (See Figure 3-7.) Discussions are held and children's thinking about student and teacher behaviors during the Daily Five is recorded on the charts. These are posted in the room so the children's thoughts and learning can be referred to all year long.

SHORT INTERVALS OF REPEATED PRACTICE

Whatever we teach, whether learning to walk down the hall correctly or learning to read independently, we were mistaken when we assumed that once shown how to do something, children would do it successfully ever after. If we provided practice time, we often made the first few practices too long or did not repeat the sessions often enough to ensure success for all.

One of the biggest influences on our practice has been Michael Grinder's work. Grinder presents how the brain receives input through three different external memory systems: visual, auditory, and kinesthetic. Once received, the input is stored by the same internal memory systems. When information is stored in more than one of these systems, the memory is improved. Memory stored in the kinesthetic system evokes the longest memory.

To activate the kinesthetic system, kinesthetic learning experiences are provided and then labeled so children hear and feel what they are doing. This movement is stored in muscle memory and becomes part of their default behaviors.

Figure 3-8 Ten Steps to Improve Muscle Memory

1. Identify what is to be taught.
2. Set a purpose and a sense of urgency.
3. Brainstorm behaviors desired using an I-chart.
4. Model most-desirable behaviors.
5. Incorrect model—least-desirable behaviors, then model most-desirable behaviors.
6. Everyone practice and build stamina (3 minutes).
7. Teacher stays out of the way.
8. Quiet signal—Come back to group.
9. Group check-in—"How did you do?"
10. Repeat 1 through 9.

In each Daily Five lesson, the class auditorally brainstorms correct behaviors on the I-chart. Then children model these behaviors in front of the class, permitting them to be seen visually. Finally the whole class practices these behaviors kinesthetically for three minutes, allowing the behaviors to be received and stored kinesthetically for all students through their muscle memories. Daily review of the I-chart, modeling of behaviors, and extending practice periods inputs and stores these behaviors in all three memory systems, therefore becoming part of the children's default behaviors.

The introduction of a Daily Five component always includes a three-minute independent practice period, which is repeated often throughout the weeklong launching phase. You may believe your students are capable of practicing for much longer than three minutes. However, a three-minute practice is part of the process of successfully preparing children for extended periods of independent work. When our older students begin this practice time, they may have the stamina and experience to stay focused for longer than three minutes. However, we still carefully watch them for any sign that their ability to stay focused is compromised. It may be three, five, or even seven minutes the first day.

Three minutes is usually enough time for each child in the room to manage with the correct behaviors. Sometimes there are kids who are unable to complete the three minutes successfully. The important thing to remember is that if a child, even one, goes off-task during the practice time, the signal should be given to stop and gather students back together to review how it went. We never want children to continue with the off-task behavior, because that means they are practicing the wrong way and training their muscle memories incorrectly. It is very difficult to change incorrect behaviors if we allow them to become ingrained.

We never set a timer for a three-minute practice, because it impedes the flexibility to change the length of time to meet our children's needs. We do not want the time to dictate when the children move; we want our children's behaviors to influence when the signal is given.

For example, if we are just a minute or so into the first practice of Read to Self and one of the students gets up and begins to walk around, we merely signal the whole class, let them know that time is up, and invite them to rejoin us in the gathering place. Even though it was not three minutes, the one student who was unable to stay in one spot gave us all she was able for that moment. We do not want to let her continue to walk around when she should be sitting and reading or she will never learn the correct independent behaviors. We absolutely do not use a punishing tone in response to that child's moving around—it was the best she could do at that time. With correct encouragement and practice we can help her build her stamina so that soon she will exhibit the correct behaviors and be able to sustain them.

When all children are successful with three minutes, one minute is added to each practice. Detailed descriptions of how time is gradually increased in practice sessions are provided in subsequent chapters.

SIGNALS AND CHECK-IN

Getting children's attention in a calm and respectful manner can make or break the tone of a classroom. When children are engaged in the work time of a Daily Five session, the last thing on their minds is stopping what they are doing to join us for checking in. Calling for the class's attention can shatter the calm tone of the room. Often we assume that children know how to rejoin the whole group in a timely manner. Many of the children are compliant enough to respond to a teacher calling them back to check in, but many students find this more than challenging for a variety of reasons.

Each year there are those few children who seem to take forever to give us their attention. We can feel our frustration growing as we wait for them to join us. We often resort to calling out to them over and over again, each time our voices getting a bit louder. Introducing one loud voice in the classroom is the quickest way to have the noise level of our room go spiraling out of control. This is why it is so important to teach children to quickly respond to a signal, so they know it is time to gather and check back in.

In our classrooms the signal we opt for is a set of chimes. The balanced melody is different enough to grab the attention of our highly kinesthetic children, but not obtrusive enough to upset our auditory children. We spend time the very first day of school teaching children how to gather when they hear the chimes and then have them practice the exact behaviors we desire when we want their attention.

We are careful to explain the signal and its purpose on the first day of the year. "Class, we want you to hear this lovely sound. [Ring the chimes.] We are going to use this sound all year when we want everyone's attention or we need to gather as a class. Let's make an anchor chart together and write down our ideas about what you think it might look like and sound like in our classroom when we ring these chimes." Each time a child volunteers an idea, write it along with the child's name on the chart.

Figure 3-9 Demonstrating the chimes' quiet signal.

Haley: "When you ring the chimes, we would look at you."
Zoe: "We should be quiet so we can hear you."
Matthew: "Yeah, 'cause my mom always says if I'm talking I can't hear very much."
Allie: "I think it would sound kinda quiet in here when you ring the chimes."

"What do you think our classroom would look like?"

Diana: "In my class last year my teacher would say, 'Stop, look and listen.' So I think that's what our class would look like."

Read back over the chart. "Boys and girls, let's practice your ideas."

At this point, we have our children get up, move around, and chat among themselves, creating a very noisy classroom. We ring the chimes, and the children exhibit the behaviors on the chart. Waiting until we have everyone's attention, we go over the chart to see how they all did, and check in (see check-in), then go back to a noisy room so we can ring the chimes and practice again. At the beginning of the school year it feels like a game. We keep it upbeat, fun, and positive, practicing four to five times in a row and varied times throughout the rest of the school day and the days that follow. Each time we practice, we stop and look over our chart, checking in to see if we have all been successful with the behaviors and adding any new behaviors as we see fit.

The signal is used throughout the year to bring students back together for check-in. One of our goals is to help children become self-reflective about their behaviors and learning. We've seen that some kids *are* naturally self-reflective, but all children can learn to become more so. Effective instruction is about developing learners who actively and independently monitor and regulate their own learning.

CHECK-IN

One way we teach children to be more self-reflective is through check-in. The use of check-in, in connection with child-generated I-charts, helps children become more aware of the expectations of the classroom culture and how successful they were as they work toward the expectations. We have children put a thumbs-up, right in front of their hearts, to signal if they knew in their hearts they were independent and successful with that behavior. We have them put a thumb sideways if they thought they were somewhat independent and successful but could do better. We tell them the thumb is only for their reflection—they shouldn't worry about classmates' signals.

Figure 3-10 Thumb Check-in

We do not have children put their thumbs down. You may have children who thrive on that negative attention. We want to send a very clear message that we are all works in progress. If their thumbs are sideways, they gave what they could and are acknowledging that they could do better. Isn't that the kind of self-reflection we want? A thumbs-down indicates that nothing was good, and we don't believe that is true. We always function under the positive presupposition that kids can and will learn.

CORRECT MODEL/INCORRECT MODEL

Eventually I realized, of course, that nothing was wrong with "these kids."
They didn't get it because I hadn't *shown them how*. I'd told them to be
respectful, thoughtful, and kind, but I hadn't shown them what that looks
and sounds like. (p. 18)

—*Debbie Miller, **Reading with Meaning:
Teaching Comprehension in the Primary Grades.***

How can we expect children to demonstrate behaviors that they have never seen, at least not in a way that has emphasized their importance? This is where the correct model/incorrect model comes in.

Modeling is a concept every teacher is familiar with, but often it doesn't receive the priority or time it deserves. Regardless of the skill being taught, we always model what the skill looks like when done properly. In the case of the Daily Five, we begin with a discussion of what the skill looks like. After this discussion, we have a student model the previously discussed attributes of the particular skill being learned. While the student demonstrates, we quietly point out to the rest of the class all of the behaviors the student is demonstrating (such as reading quietly, staying in one spot, finishing a book and beginning another one, and reading the entire time).

Next comes our twist on the familiar modeling scenario. We call this the incorrect model. What we know about some of our more challenging students is that their behavior is often a call for attention. We ask for someone to volunteer to model the incorrect way. Often there is a student who is going to want to use the Daily Five as a time to act out in an effort to get attention, so we give him or her an audience right up front

Figure 3-11a Incorrect Model of Read to Self

Figure 3-11b Correct Model of Read to Self

when we are able to shape his or her behaviors. So, for this modeling, we choose one of our more challenging students, one who will want the attention of doing this the incorrect way. This is an opportunity to point out behaviors that we want to discourage.

The other children find this modeling the wrong way very entertaining, but the second part of correct model/incorrect model is where the deep learning occurs. After demonstrating all the things the child shouldn't do, we ask the student to model the appropriate behaviors. Again we point out all the positive behavior being modeled. The child enjoys the positive attention just as much as the laughter generated by the inappropriate choices. This challenging student has now shown us, all the other children in the class, and most important himself or herself, that he or she is able to exhibit the behavior appropriately and receive positive attention in doing so, and be held accountable for it.

This kind of correct model/incorrect model interaction is very powerful. Through this kind of practice, all children realize they are able to do the Daily Five with appropriate behaviors. By seeing what's expected and what is unacceptable, they have a much clearer idea of what they are to do as well as what they should *not* be doing. The latter can often be more important, because it clarifies and further delineates the boundaries of acceptability within the classroom. When problems occur (and they will), gentle reminders affirm the students by letting them know that we believe they can do it. These reminders help all the children develop the correct behaviors for each skill.

Correct model/incorrect model addresses the visual input of correct behaviors for the whole class and the kinesthetic input for those modeling, thus beginning the process of creating children's muscle memories.

The beginning of the year is all about establishing routines, defining expectations, practicing behaviors, and building stamina with children within the Daily Five framework, and it takes lots of discipline on the children's part as well as the teacher's. We move slowly to eventually move fast. The payoff is enormous.

Now we go into the specifics of how each of the Daily Five elements is launched in the first weeks of school.

PART II

The Daily Five in Action

04

READ TO SELF

■ ■ ■ ■ ■

Just adding more time and space for independent reading is not enough. I'm advocating a carefully designed, structured reading program that includes demonstrating, teaching, guiding, monitoring, evaluating, and goal setting along with voluntary reading of books students choose. . . . When an independent reading component is added, test scores go up.

—*Regie Routman*

■ ■ ■ ■ ■

Upon completion of kindergarten, five-year-old Ben was reflecting on his year. When asked what most helped him become a reader, he promptly replied, "Daily Five, 'cause when I do Read to Self I get more better at reading." We asked him to explain why Read to Self helped him become a better reader. He slowly cocked his head to the left, looked up at the ceiling, and began to speak in his deliberate, eloquent, five-year-old manner. "Well, when I do Read to Self, I get to work on my accuracy. When I came to school, I couldn't read the words right, but I practiced every day during Daily Five and now I can read."

Having children read to themselves is the first step in Daily Five and is the foundation for creating independent readers and writers. On the surface—like all of the components in Daily Five—Read to Self seems basic and simple. However, we have found that specific teaching techniques can make Read to Self a powerful tool for enhancing all literacy skills. When fully implemented, Read to Self involves a number of deliberate and planned actions throughout the day. But as with learning (or teaching) any new skill, the key to successful implementation of Read to Self and Daily Five is to start with small steps and build as you go.

The launching of each component of the Daily Five is based upon the "gradual release of responsibility" model by Pearson and Gallagher (1983). Harvey and Goudvis (2000) describe this model in *Strategies That Work* as "teaching a strategy by modeling for the whole class, guiding students in its practice in small groups and pairs and providing large blocks of time for students to read independently and practice using and applying the strategy. . . . All instruction is geared toward children using these strategies independently, applying them if and when they need them" (p. 12–13).

It's hard to find any book written recently in literacy that doesn't advocate the use of the gradual release of responsibility model. But when it comes to actual practice, we often made the mistake of thinking that if we taught students something and gave them an opportunity to practice it once or twice, they were ready to work on their own. That's why, as we present each component of the Daily Five, you will see that we have taken the "gradual" in "gradual release" to heart in our teaching. We work with students to describe a new skill or behavior together, model it, practice it, talk about the skill again, and repeat the practice and discussion until the behavior becomes a habit. As you read our description of the first Daily Five, Read to Self, you will notice that each launching session includes multiple short practice sessions, with repetition and discussion throughout the first weeks of school. We have found that this repetition is the key to success in helping students develop good literacy habits and independence.

We have introduced hundreds of teachers to the Daily Five since 1996, and the overwhelming majority have experienced success with it in their own classrooms. In the few cases where the program has failed, it has invariably been because there was little modeling of the new skills and a lack of repeated practice.

The tone for the entire year is established during the early weeks of school. When we take our time during this critically important period, moving slowly and thoughtfully to build a solid foundation, it pays off all year long.

LAUNCHING READ TO SELF

We start the first day of Read to Self by gathering the class on the floor in front of us (yes, on the floor, no matter what grade level we teach). The easel is by our side, ready to capture the class's thinking and ideas. The children's book boxes have been filled and stand at attention against the wall. It is time to begin by teaching our first lesson, "Three Ways to Read a Book."

THREE WAYS TO READ A BOOK

One of the first concepts we teach is that there are three ways to read a book. Students are honored as learners, whatever their stage of reading development, when they understand that readers may do any of the following:

- ■ Read and talk about the pictures
- ■ Read the words
- ■ Retell a previously read book

Whether the students are very young, learning English, struggling learners, or highly gifted, this understanding is essential if they are to read independently for extended periods of time.

"Three Ways to Read a Book" is taught in two sessions that look like this. On the first day, we start with these words: "Today, class, we are going to learn two ways to read a book. Who knows what those ways are? Guy?"

"One way is to read the words."

"That is right! We read the words to understand what is happening in the book. What is another way to read?"

The class usually stares blankly or restates "reading the words" in various ways.

Sometimes, a lone voice tentatively asks, "Read the pictures?"

"Yes, pictures often carry much of a story's meaning, so it is really important to read them."

This new thinking is empowering to our youngest or most inexperienced students who until now have believed that reading means the words or nothing at all.

"You are going to be detectives today and notice what it looks like and sounds like when we read a book two different ways.

"First, we will read a book using just the pictures. Pay close attention so you can turn and tell an elbow buddy what you saw and heard when I'm through."

We always start with reading pictures. It is often intriguing for the children because this can be the first time they have ever heard that reading the pictures is reading. Many will say "I do that" after hearing us read the pictures, but still can't believe it is really reading. However, much of learning to read, especially in the beginning stages, is a combination of reading the words, cross-checking with the pictures, and making meaning of the story.

Using a picture book (this lesson works best with an emergent-level book with few words, and pictures that carry most of the story's meaning) we model reading the pictures by talking or commenting about each picture in the book. We tell the story, modeling the same metacognitive process to think about our reading and comprehension as we do when we are reading the words. It's okay if our words don't match the text or story, as long as they can be supported by the pictures.

When finished with the story, we say, "Reading the pictures is one way of reading a story. Boys and girls, what did you notice us doing?" (Some common responses involve looking at the pictures, talking about the pictures, thinking, making meaning, and having fun.) We respond, "You are great detectives! Now, see if you can tell what is the same and what is different after I read you the words of this book."

We read the same story using the text, again modeling the metacognitive process of thinking aloud about our reading and comprehension that we will soon expect students to replicate. At the end of our reading we say, "This was a second way to read a story— reading the words. Okay, detectives, what did you notice?" (Again, they may mention looking at the words and pictures, talking, thinking, and having fun.)

"You guys are so smart! Whether you read the words, pictures, or both together, you should be thinking, talking to yourself, and making meaning. Your brain will be very busy when you are reading!"

These observations have become part of our collective learning, forming new background knowledge that will transfer to their independent practice.

On the second day, we begin by reviewing the previous day's learning: "Please put a thumb in the air if you remember the two ways to read a book that we learned about yesterday." Many thumbs go up. "Please turn and tell your elbow buddy one of the ways, and see if he or she can remember the other way.

"Great! I heard 'read the words' and 'read the pictures'. Today, we are going to look at one last way to read a book, and that is 'retelling a story I read before.' This is the book I read to you yesterday. Because I read you the words and the pictures, it is still pretty fresh in my mind, so watch closely and I'll show you what it looks like and sounds like when you retell."

We go through the book page by page, retelling the book with much detail. Once again we model the strategies that we expect of children, the

Figure 4-1 Focus Lesson on Three Ways to Read a Book

metacognitive process of thinking aloud about our reading and comprehension.

"Did you notice that I used the pictures and what I remembered from reading the words to retell the story? It is a fun way to read a book, especially a favorite book! Today, when you build your stamina in Read-to-Self time, you may choose to read the words or the pictures, or retell a book you already read."

It is essential to teach what it looks and sounds like to read the pictures, read the words, and retell. When children understand the three ways and the thinking that goes along with each, they will be able to practice effectively, becoming independent at reading for extended periods of time.

LAUNCHING READ TO SELF

We then begin our explanation of the Daily Five by launching the Read-to-Self component of the program. "Today we are going to begin our very first day of the Daily Five. We know that the most important thing we can do to become better readers who love to read is to spend lots of time practicing reading. Let's begin by making an I-chart, with our ideas of why it is so important that we read to ourselves."

On top of the I-chart we write the heading "Read to Self, Independence." Under the heading, we write "Why: to become a better reader."

We continue, "That is why we will begin Daily Five with Read to Self. Why else do we read to ourselves?" As the children respond, we write their ideas on the chart.

Kelsey: "Because it's fun!"
Scott: "I can learn interesting things."
Lynn: "It can take me places."
Jolie: "Because I love to read!"

We add an *I,* which we explain to students stands for *Independence,* to the Read-to-Self anchor chart. We write "students" on the top left and "teacher" on the top right.

Calling on a child to get us started, we brainstorm appropriate Read-to-Self behaviors. "Emily, if our class were to do Read to Self independently, which means all by yourselves, what do you think it might look, sound, or feel like?" We record students' thinking on the chart along with their names.

Emily: "We wouldn't hear a lot of noise."
Matthew: "We would see kids sitting around the room looking at books."

One idea students may not mention is "reading the whole time." It is vital that this idea be added to the I-chart. Many of us know that some of our most reluctant readers are masters of "reading avoidance," which Cris Tovani describes so clearly in *I Read It but I Don't Get It* (2000). They start out with a book, but all too quickly are up and moving about the room. They may be sharpening their pencils, getting a drink, going to the bathroom, shopping for new books—anything to avoid reading. This behavior can be one of the most detrimental to our most struggling readers.

We extend the conversation to talk about our roles as the teachers:

"These are all such good ideas. You already know a lot about how Read to Self looks, feels, and sounds. What about the teacher? What would the teacher be doing?"

Haley: "I think you would be reading, too."
Emily: "You might be working on the computer."
Peter: "I think you would work with kids."

Figure 4-2 Read-to-Self I-chart

Students	Teacher
■ Read the whole time. Matthew	■ Work with groups of students
■ Stay in one spot. Jenna	■ Listen to children read
■ Read quietly. Karyn	■ Help students with reading
■ Work on stamina. Scott	
■ Get started right away. Michelle	

We add "teacher" to the I-chart because we want the children to know we also have a job. It is fascinating to see what they think we will be doing. We make sure to add the following statements to the "teacher" side of the I-chart: read with groups of children, read with children one at a time, listen to children read, and help them with their reading strategies.

After completing the I-chart, we move into modeling. We ask the class, "Now that we have talked about what Read to Self might look like, sound like, and feel like, is there anyone who would like to model, or show the class?"

We choose a person to model the behaviors of Read to Self. The student gets his or her book box, goes to the front of the group, sits down, takes out the first book, and begins to read.

While the student models we quietly go over the chart with the rest of the class.

"Let's look at Benjamin as he models for us. Wow, he is certainly staying in one spot." We point to the I-chart while observing each behavior as Benjamin models Read to Self. "Can you see him staying focused on the book? Oh, now look, he has finished that book and is putting it back into his book box and taking out another. Good for him—he is not stopping his reading just because his first book is done; he is going on to another book so he is reading the whole time." We end with a round of applause for Benjamin.

We ask, "Who can tell us what you saw Benjamin doing as he was practicing Read to Self?" As children relate what they saw, we point out these behaviors on the I-chart. We might also choose a few other students to model in front of the class, following the example above.

The next step in launching Read to Self is choosing an incorrect model (see Chapter 3). We find a student to model Read to Self the "inappropriate" way.

"Is there anyone who would like to model Read to Self the inappropriate way? Travis? Do you think you can do it wrong?" We have already figured out that Travis is a student who will want the attention of doing this the inappropriate way, so we choose him to model the inappropriate behaviors in front of the whole class. Travis grabs his book box and goes to the front of the class, already laughing and dancing.

"Okay, let's watch Travis as he models Read to Self the inappropriate way." Travis begins his antics by picking up one book from his book box, throwing it down, and grabbing another. "Oh my, let's look at our chart." (We point to the I-chart.) "Is he staying focused on his book?" Amid giggles and laughter, the whole class is thrilled to chime in that he is not. We exclaim, "Goodness, look at Travis now." Travis has gotten up and is charging to the water fountain. Pointing to the chart we ask, "Is Travis staying in one spot? Oh, no!" On his way back from the fountain, he is yelling across the room to two other students. Pointing to the chart, we ask students in the class another question relating to the brainstormed ideas they generated earlier. We ask, "Is Travis reading quietly? Oh, no!" Travis is thrilled with the attention.

Next is when magic occurs. "Okay, Travis, now please show us the appropriate way to Read to Self." Travis quickly settles in, just as he had watched the other children model. He is enjoying this positive attention as much as the laughter he generated from the inappropriate choices. Pointing to the chart we ask, "Wow, look at Travis. Is he staying in one spot? How about reading the whole time? Is he staying focused on the book?" In fact, because Travis has seen the other children model Read to Self correctly, he is able to model just as they did.

This interaction has been powerful. In front of the teacher and all the students, Travis has proved that he is absolutely able to do Read to Self with the correct behaviors listed on our class I-chart. If Travis chooses not to exhibit the correct behaviors as students move to Read to Self, we can gently remind him of his success, confirm that we know he can do it, and continue to help form his behaviors.

PRACTICING READ TO SELF—
THE THREE-MINUTE START

Next, we move to the practice phase of the lesson.

We redirect the students with the following: "We are ready to have you all practice Read to Self. Each of you has a book box. Right now you are going to find out where children in our class sit during Read to Self. Then we will practice Read to Self, for just three minutes."

Groans from the class are punctuated by "We can do it much longer!" "How about twenty minutes?"

We respond, "The reason we are practicing for just three minutes is that we are working to help you build your stamina and to train your bodies and brains to do Read to Self the appropriate way, the

Figure 4-3 Children are placed around the room for Read to Self.

ways we brainstormed on the chart and the way you saw some of your friends model. Building your stamina each day will help you all year long as we work toward becoming better readers who love to read."

At this time, we quickly and quietly take children with their book boxes, one at a time, and place them around the room at least an arm's distance away from each other. This activity looks different in each classroom, depending on its setup. We guide children the first few days because we are teaching them to make thoughtful choices about where to sit. Each classroom is arranged differently, and each teacher has different comfort levels for where children spend time reading in their room. In our classrooms, we show children that they can sit almost anywhere: on the floor with a big pillow, under a table, on the couch, on a chair at a table, in the rocker in the class den, and so forth. They may also choose to lie on the rug in the middle of the room.

The reason for a three-minute practice is that most children can be successful for that amount of time. When training children's muscle memories, it is crucial that they practice with correct behaviors. As soon as someone is unable to focus on his or her book or stay in one spot, it is time to stop. The advantage of teaching in primary grades is that we can tell them that three minutes is up and call them back to the gathering place whether three minutes have passed or not. Because most cannot tell time, they don't realize that we stopped early!

The children have brainstormed the Read-to-Self behaviors, seen them modeled, and are set up around the classroom. They know we will be practicing for three minutes. At this time we sit at our guided reading or assessment spot, out of the way of children's reading. We do not manage by proximity or even make eye contact.

Figure 4-4 Children practice Read to Self in comfortable places.

CHECKING BACK IN

After about three minutes, we signal the class back to the gathering space in our room for a check-in.

We direct their attention again to the I-chart: "Let's look over our I-chart of Read to Self and reflect on how it went. As we read through each of the items on the chart, think about your Read-to-Self behaviors. Were you practicing what readers who Read to Self do? Put your closed hand right next to your heart. As we go through each Read-to-Self behavior on our chart, think about how you did today. If you know in your heart that you were successful today, put your thumb up. If in your heart you know that you can improve in that area, put your thumb sideways. Keep it close to you, right next to your heart."

We read over the items on the student side of the chart, one at a time, giving enough time for each child to reflect.

We continue the discussion by asking, "Is there anyone who would like to share a celebration of what went well during our first practice?"

Zoe: "I was sitting close to Ingrid, and even though we were near each other, I was able to read the whole time because she was not bothering me."
Jacob: "I had enough books to read the whole time!"
Jolie: "I was really cozy and didn't want to quit. I was right in the middle of reading the pictures in my book. Can't we do it longer?"

We ask, "Before we practice again, are there any changes you think we need to make?"

Diana: "I need to sit somewhere else. I wasn't comfortable on the floor."
Doug: "Travis was bothering me the whole time, so I couldn't read."

We invite Doug into a problem-solving discussion with Travis. "Doug, what do you think you might want to say to Travis?"

Because Travis was one of the students who modeled inappropriate Daily Five behaviors and then correct behaviors, all the kids, including Doug, are aware that Travis knows the right ones.

Doug responds, "Travis, you were bothering me! When you were talking to me, hitting me with your foot, and making those funny sounds, you were interrupting my reading. I saw you do it the right way. Could you please try?"

"Great words, Doug. You know, class, Read to Self is the very best way to become a better reader. When we bother others during this time, we are not allowing them or ourselves the chance to practice our reading and become better readers."

THREE MORE MINUTES OF PRACTICE AND CHECK-IN

Next, we try one more practice and check-in, allowing children to revise the I-chart before we begin. "We are going to do another three-minute practice. Let's look one more time at our I-chart before we go. Is there anything we need to add to this chart to help make our Read-to-Self time go even better?"

Kelsey responds, "I think we shouldn't sit too close to each other. Otherwise we might want to chat or bother others' reading time."

"Wise thinking, Kelsey. Any other ideas?"

Once again, we take each child and their book box and place them in a different place around the room. It is important that children not always sit in the same spot when we are training their muscle memories, because doing so might anchor their good behavior to that certain spot. Having children experience success in places throughout the room will set them up for positive results wherever they choose to sit as the year goes on. During this practice time, we note that Travis has more success. We will continue to be aware of his level of engagement and independent behaviors. After three minutes or as soon as necessary, we signal students to return to the whole group.

We again ask students to reflect. "Let's talk about how that three-minute practice of Read to Self went. Who would like to share something that went well?"

Doug responds, "Travis, you did GREAT! I didn't hear you at all, so I could read the whole time. Thanks!"

Travis breaks into a huge grin.

Jenna: "I read the pictures of five books in my book box!"
Kalen: "I didn't want to quit."

We review the I-chart again, with students using their thumbs to reflect upon their behaviors. This reflection helps them set their goals for the next practice. This practice and reflection process can be used just once on the first day or repeated as many as three or four times. Our schedule and the children's stamina determine these practice times.

REVIEW THE LESSON

Finally, we review the lesson after all these practice sessions.

"We just learned about the first part of Daily Five called Read to Self. What did you learn about why we do Read to Self, and how we do Read to Self?"

Brianne responds, "It is the best way to get to be a better reader."

Kamar adds, "We stay in one spot and read the whole time."

Dean says, "We do it more every day so we can build our st— st—, what is that word?"

"Dean, *stamina* is the word you are looking for. We will add more time each day so we can build our stamina."

We continue asking children to review the most important parts of their Daily Five with help from the I-chart when necessary.

Reviewing a lesson summarizes for students the key points of the day's learning, enabling them to more readily remember the important parts. Telling children what they will learn the next day gets them excited and prepares their brains for what comes next. The review process lets them know that reflection is ongoing. It builds background knowledge and experiences, allowing them to connect their schema to new learning each day.

DAY TWO AND BEYOND

Day Two of Read to Self closely resembles Day One. We continue to work on building stamina and training children's muscle memories. We begin literacy time with a review of yesterday's lesson, "Three Ways to Read a Book."

Once the review of "Three Ways to Read a Book" is completed, it is time to focus on Read to Self. It's similar to the first lesson, the biggest change being an additional minute of practice time. We spend time each day reviewing the I-charts, because these charts will guide our learning throughout the year.

We read over each item the class generated on yesterday's chart, pausing long enough for children to form pictures in their minds.

We choose one to three students to come to the front of the group with their book boxes and model Read to Self, just as we did on Day One.

Reflecting on yesterday, we always ask ourselves if any of the children had a difficult time with the behaviors of Read to Self during the three-minute practice. These would be good candidates to choose when asking if anyone would like to model Read to Self in the least-preferred way, and then have them model the most-preferred way.

As on Day One of starting Daily Five, children and their book boxes are placed around the room according to the comfort level of the teacher and each child, whether that means sitting under a table, lying on his or her stomach, sitting at a table, curling up in a corner, sitting on a couch, or something else.

We are gradually adding time in our effort to support children as they build their stamina for exhibiting the appropriate behaviors for Read to Self.

While students are practicing Read to Self, we continue to stay out of the way of their reading. This means no eye contact or managing by proximity. We make a point of sitting at the guided reading or assessment spot.

After the four-minute practice, we signal students to meet again as a whole group and check in. How did it go? We review the I-chart from Day One.

At any time, if students are not able to sustain the correct behaviors of Read to Self, we signal them to return to the whole group.

After the four-minute practice of Read to Self and whole-group check-in, having children model in front of the whole class is discretionary. Modeling the appropriate and inappropriate behaviors takes place on the first day of introducing Read to Self, and the start of the second day, but then becomes optional. If children seem to be successful with the Read-to-Self behaviors, it is now a matter of slowly building their stamina. We find that if children are still having difficulty with the behaviors, they need to see it modeled by others and to model it themselves (both the inappropriate and appropriate ways).

We continue the process of reviewing the behaviors on the I-chart, placing children around the room with their book boxes, practicing, and returning to the whole group to check on how it went. We practice three or four times so we can help build their muscle memories.

If children are having difficulty with Read-to-Self behaviors, we stop, reflect, and question. Is it due to a lack of stamina or to not knowing the on-task behaviors? If children's difficulty with Read to Self is caused by lack of stamina, we maintain the number of minutes and increase the number of practice sessions each day. If, however, their difficulty stems from not performing on-task behaviors, we add to the I-chart, review "Sense of Urgency," and model more extensively the appropriate behaviors.

Having children invest high-quality time in this process now will provide greater benefits and results as the year progresses. After taking one of our courses, a team of four teachers from our area were sharing with great exuberance how independent their students had become since the implementation of Daily Five in their classrooms. As the four reflected on the reasons for this high level of independence, they concluded that they had launched each element of the Daily Five by modeling it again and again in the first weeks. Kids then took control of the modeling, and this ensured success.

Seeing the desired behaviors modeled over and over solidified the expected behaviors for all students. "It was hard to model so many times," explained one teacher. "It wasn't what I was used to."

As Cris Tovani notes, "Whenever an activity fails, it is because I haven't done enough modeling. Modeling gives students words and examples to frame their thinking" (2000, p. 82).

Throughout the first month of school, we add one to two minutes each day to Read to Self, building children's stamina until they are reading for the desired length of time. Our goal is for students to be able to read for thirty to forty-five uninterrupted minutes while exhibiting the appropriate Read-to-Self behaviors. It is during this phase that we begin teaching the independent behaviors of Read to Someone and Listen to Reading, the two components of the Daily Five we present in the next chapter.

Figure 4-5 Focus Lessons for Read to Self

Day 1
- Model "Three Ways to Read a Book."
- Brainstorm I-chart.
- Model and practice student behaviors of Read to Self.
- Begin building stamina—3 minutes.

Day 2
- Model and practice "Three Ways to Read a Book."
- Review I-chart.
- Model and practice student behaviors of Read to Self.
- Continue building stamina—4 minutes.

Day 3
- Discuss where to sit and how to choose where to sit.
- Continue with above, adding 1–2 minutes each day, extending stamina.

Day 4
- Continue to review I-chart.
- Teach how to choose good-fit books.

Once a focus lesson is taught, students Read to Self and continue to build stamina.

Add a few minutes each day until primary students are up to 30 minutes and intermediate students can sustain for up to 45 minutes.

05

READ TO SOMEONE AND LISTEN TO READING

■■■■■

We need a definite purpose, a specific reason for listening, otherwise we don't pay attention and don't really hear or understand.

—*Robert Montgomery*

■■■■■

We recently ran into a woman at an Internet café who asked why we were there. After we shared that we were writing a book on reading, she said passionately, "You have got to get those families to read to their kids! I volunteer in an elementary school, and those kids need more time with books." We couldn't agree more about the value of reading outside of school, yet we don't have control over that realm of a child's experience and education. Instead of complaining about how poverty or mobility affects our students and their parents (who may be more focused on where their next meal is coming from than a bedtime story), we think of Hopkin's (2002) words, "Teachers have no control over which students walk into their classes, what goes on outside school, or other external factors, but teachers can control how they react to those things that happen. Throughout my 30-plus years in education, I have seen master teachers who always maintain a positive attitude toward teaching and learning—and they always get results."

One way to give children additional exposure to books is to increase the amount of time they hear fluent and expressive reading by others. This can take place in many forms during the day: read-aloud, shared reading, guided reading, partner reading, cross-age buddies, or books on tape.

In this chapter, we present the second and third components of the Daily Five, Read to Someone and Listen to Reading. Read to Someone helps children learn to collaborate and be flexible with peers. Listen to Reading is the Daily Five component that enables students to listen to stories on tape or CDs.

READ TO SOMEONE

Reading with someone helps students read independently and grow as readers. Reading with someone helps readers, especially developing readers, become more self-sufficient and less reliant on the teacher for assistance. Research shows that taking turns reading increases reading involvement, attention, and collaboration. What's more, kids love partner reading and readily do it with books of their choosing.

Of all the sessions children participate in, Read to Someone becomes a favorite of most, and why not? They have a friend to read and discuss books with, and to share thinking and learning with. In addition, it increases the following:

- The volume of reading
- The level of attention to reading
- Reading motivation
- Fluency
- Reading rate
- Word-attack skills
- The love of reading

Some teachers, believing in the benefits, have tried partner reading only to feel frustrated with the noise level and accountability issue. We'll share a few strategies that will enable your students to derive the benefits from partner reading and enable you to not only maintain your sanity, but enjoy this session as well.

Although Read to Someone follows the same teaching format as the other elements of the Daily Five, it has a few extra components that ensure its success. If you take time to introduce and teach the behaviors of Read to Someone, your children will become independent and it will be well worth your investment of time.

INTRODUCING READ TO SOMEONE

When we tell our students that we are going to introduce the Read to Someone component of the Daily Five, cheers go up in the classroom. Friends sitting near each other on the floor typically throw their arms around each other's necks, exclaiming, "I can't WAIT to read with you!" One child squeals to another. Three boys start punching each other's arms. Two little ones toward the back have moved to their knees and are bouncing up and down and clapping. It all comes flashing back. "This is why we hated to have children read to each other for so many years!" But we know the exuberance is merely a reflection of the joy of reading with a friend, and that explicit teaching and practice will lead to engaged and productive partnerships instead of chaos.

We pose the important opening question, "Why do you suppose we would want to read to someone every day?" Hands shoot into the air; children on the back of the rug are bouncing around, and a chorus of voices sings out, "Because it's fun!"

"It certainly is fun! What would be another reason to spend our very precious time each day reading to someone?"

The answers that follow range from "We make good friends" to "So we aren't lonely." Quickly someone offers, "So we can become better readers?"

"Yes!" we respond, matching their exuberance. "Because fun and getting better at reading are two of the most important reasons we read to someone. There are a couple of other reasons as well. Any ideas?" At this point we usually put on the chart "It helps us with our fluency" and "We can practice our reading skills and strategies."

"Remember each day as we read to you we have been showing you how it sounds when fluent readers read and how it sounds when someone is not reading fluently? Practicing your fluency is another one of the reasons we read to someone. It is also going to be a time when you get to practice the skills and reading strategies you are learning in class."

What we've found matters most for the success of Read to Someone is presenting a series of lessons during the first six days that takes students step-by-step through the skills they will need to listen carefully to their peers, offer assistance, and share materials fairly.

The explicit teaching and practicing of these skills has made all the difference in the quality of the social interactions our students have as they read with partners.

Figure 5-1 Focus Lessons for Read to Someone

Day 1
- Model and practice EEKK (elbow, elbow, knee, knee), voice level, and "Check for Understanding."
  - "I just heard you read . . ." (who, what)
- Brainstorm I-chart.

Day 2
- Model and practice how partners read.
  - Both read same book—"I Read, You Read"
    - Partner not reading checks for understanding. Switch jobs after each page or paragraph.
  - Each choose own book and read a page; partner checks for understanding.
    - Two different books are being read by partners.

Day 3
- Brainstorm and practice "How to Choose Books."
  - Talk about it and make a deal.
  - Rock, paper, scissors

Day 4
- Brainstorm and practice where to sit in room.

Day 5
- Model and practice "How to Choose a Partner."
  - Raise your hand as a silent signal that you need a partner.
  - Make eye contact with another person who has his or her hand raised.
  - Walk to the person and say, "Do you want to be my partner?"
  - Partner says, "Sure."

Day 6
- Model and practice "Coaching or Time."
  - If a partner comes to a word they don't know, the other partner:
    - Counts silently to 3.
    - Asks, "Do you want coaching or time?"
      - If coaching, they use clues to help partner.
      - If time, sit patiently and wait.

Once a focus lesson is taught, students read to someone and build stamina.

Each day add a few more minutes until they are up to 30 minutes for primary students and 45 minutes for intermediate students.

FOCUS LESSON DAY 1: EEKK, VOICE, CHECK

We always begin with EEKK, an acronym that our students love. "Before we brainstorm the behaviors of Read to Someone, we'd like to teach you a couple of tricks for being good reading partners. We want to tell you a little story. As you know, my sister doesn't like spiders. What do you suppose she says and does when she sees a spider?"

"I scream, so I bet she screams!" replies Haley.

"She sure does. She says EEKK!" On the chart paper we write the letters *EEKK,* one under the other down the left side. "And then do you know what she does? She moves over, really close to me. She sits elbow to elbow, knee to knee, right beside me." On the chart paper, we write "Elbow, Elbow" by the two *E*'s and "Knee, Knee" by the two *K*'s. "Haley, would you come sit right up here beside me and pretend you are my sister who has just seen a spider?" Haley and I sit on the floor right next to each other, so that our elbows and knees are lined up, almost touching. Having children sit this way allows for easier book sharing and partner coaching. I pick up a book and put it between Haley and me so she is holding one side of the book and I am holding the other.

Figure 5-2 Read-to-Someone Definitions

EEKK—Elbow to Elbow, Knee to Knee
During Read to Someone, students sit right next to each other, almost close enough to touch elbows and knees. This close proximity allows for children to read quietly and still be heard by their partners but not loud enough for the rest of the class to hear. This sitting arrangement allows partners to look on and read the same book if they choose.

I Read, You Read
One student reads a page or a paragraph, then the partner reads the next page or paragraph. A variation on this strategy is to have one person read a paragraph and the partner read the same paragraph. This second strategy is especially useful when working on fluency. The more fluent readers read first. The less fluent readers are able to hear the pace, intonation, and correct words so they can read like their partners.

Choral Read
Partners read the same section of the book at the same time, a useful strategy to support challenged readers if they are partnered with someone who is just a step ahead of them in their reading.

Reading One Book
One book is shared between the partnership, with both students holding a corner of the book. Students take turns reading from the same book.

Figure 5-2 Read-to-Someone Definitions *(continued)*

Reading Different Books
Each student in the pair holds a different book. Students take turns reading from their books while their partners listen and check for understanding. At a designated stopping point the children who are reading stop and listen intently to their partners as they read a section from their books. When they are finished, the partners check for understanding and the reading continues.

Check for Understanding
This comprehension strategy is used to help children self-monitor the meaning of what they are reading. When reading to self, children stop at the end of each sentence, page, or paragraph and summarize what was just read by saying, for example, "I just read that Goldilocks arrived at a house and is sitting in all the chairs." If children are reading to someone, one partner reads out loud while the other holds a check mark (see Figure 5.3) and checks for understanding. When their partner comes to the end of a sentence, page, or paragraph, depending on the length of the book, the partner with the check mark says, "I just heard you read . . . the three bears found Goldilocks and she ran out of the house."

VOICE LEVEL

After modeling how to hold the book, we talk about voice level. "See how easy it is for the two of us to share a book when we sit this way? Listen how quiet our voices can be when we sit this close." We begin to read to Haley in a very soft voice. "Haley, can you hear me even though I am reading to you in a very soft voice?" The often gregarious and loud Haley merely nods. The soft voice we use influences the volume of her response. "Ben, you are sitting the farthest from us. Can you hear my voice as I read to Haley?" The volume of our voices influences him as well, and he whispers, "No."

Michael Grinder has helped us understand that the loudest voice in the room is the one that regulates the noise level. Therefore we purposefully model a very soft voice when we show children how to read to someone. When we do correct model/incorrect model, we reinforce this expectation as well. We continue this example throughout the year as we quietly confer with children during the Daily Five. We don't want our voices to be the loudest in the room!

CHECK FOR UNDERSTANDING

We close this opening day's lesson by demonstrating how to check for understanding. "Think back to the picture books I have been reading to you. Put your thumb up if you remember seeing and hearing me stop at the end of every page or so to try to remember who I was reading about and what was happening."

José: "I remember that. You called it Check for Understanding."

"That's right José." We start a new anchor chart titled "Ways to Read to Someone" and add "Check for Understanding" under the title. "Whenever we read, we stop to check for understanding, even when we read to someone. Let me show you what that would look like. José will you help me?" José joins me on the floor. "Turn to an elbow buddy and tell them how partners sit when they are doing Read to Someone." As the partners talk, José and I move into Read-to-Someone position (EEKK) with the book *The Three Bears* between us. "Turn to a different elbow buddy and tell them what kind of voice we use when we read to someone."

We tell the students that we will read along with our eyes and ears, because when José is finished with the first page, we will be checking for understanding. "José, would you start Read to Someone and read the first page of this book?" After he reads, we hold up a wooden check mark that says "Check for Understanding." We explain that the check mark reminded us to listen to José so that when he was finished, we could check for understanding by summarizing what he read. "José, I just heard you read that there were three bears who lived in a forest and they were going to eat their porridge for breakfast, but it was too hot. So they decided to go for a walk to let it cool down."

José indicates that this is correct. "Now, boys and girls, we are going to switch jobs. I am going to read and José is going to check for understanding." After we read the next page, José checks for the "who" and "what" in the story. We switch roles again, but we do not correctly summarize the gist of the reading. José responds, "That's not what I read."

Figure 5-3 Check for Understanding

We explain to the class, "José told me that I did not understand and remember what he just read. If that happens, José rereads the page. This time I listen very carefully, trying to remember what he just read so I can check for understanding." José rereads the page, and this time I summarize it correctly.

Then students are asked to tell an elbow buddy what the listener's job is when the reader is reading.

I-CHART, MODELING, PRACTICE, AND CHECK-IN

After modeling we create an I-chart. We ask, "If a visitor were to walk into our classroom and see us reading to someone independently, what might they see you and I doing?" We record each thought, placing the child's name beside it.

Aldo: "I think we would be sitting EEKK, like we just saw a spider!"
Michelle: "Yeah, and that means elbow to elbow, knee to knee."
Karyn: "We would be holding check marks and checking for understanding with our partners."
Emilio: "I think it should be just like Read to Self. We should stay in one spot and even keep our book boxes with us." (Emilio is our consummate organizer!)
Ben: "Hey, guys, don't forget, we gotta read the whole time!"
Diana: "Remember the soft voice? We have to use soft voices."

"Boys and girls, what do you think I will be doing?" We seldom hear "working on your computer" or "correcting papers" like we did the very first time we posed this question, but if we do get answers like that, we don't include them on the chart. The only item that goes up on the teacher side is "Work with students."

Figure 5-4 Read-to-Someone I-Chart

Read to Someone

Urgency:
■ Helps us become better readers
■ Best way to practice fluency
■ It is fun.

Sample I-Chart
Read to Someone
Independence

Students	*Teacher*
■ Sit EEKK.	■ Work with students.
■ Use a soft voice.	
■ Read the whole time.	
■ Stay in one spot.	
■ Get started right away.	

We remind students that when they are working on Read to Self and Read to Someone independently, we are teaching small groups or working with individual students.

At this time one to three sets of partners are chosen to come to the front of the group with their book boxes and model the correct behaviors of Read to Someone. This follows the same modeling pattern as in Read to Self.

The next children to model are those whom we think will have difficulty with the correct behaviors for Read to Someone. They first model Read to Someone with undesirable behaviors, and then with desirable behaviors.

Then quickly but quietly, we call two children at a time, have them grab their book boxes, and place them in a variety of locations to practice for three minutes together. We usually take this practice time to sit in a space in the room where we will later work with individuals or small groups. We refrain from the temptation to reinforce good behavior.

Once three to four minutes have gone by (or earlier if someone goes off-task), the signal is given to have kids assemble in the gathering place. The Read-to-Someone behavior chart is reviewed and we discuss any behaviors that should be added. Students use their thumbs as they reflect on each aspect and set goals for their next practice.

We repeat the correct model/incorrect model as necessary during the next couple of days.

Figure 5-5a and 5-5b Students practice reading the pictures and reading the words with their partners, sitting EEKK.

SELF-SELECTED WORK AREAS

When we first began developing the Daily Five, we would seat our most challenging children in places around the room that we deemed "safe," places where we could keep a clear eye on them and that had very few distractions or hiding places. We realized we were not doing those children any favors, for as soon as they had the opportunity to self-select where to sit, they chose the places we had been working so hard to keep them out of!

Now when launching each of the Daily Five we purposefully place challenging children in those places that may seem risky, but will surely be chosen if the opportunity arises (a loft, den, or carpeted floor area). We believe that given choice, some may initially practice undesirable behaviors but they will quickly see the value in practicing appropriate ones and build their stamina by doing so.

Gathering the children back on the rug, we close our first day of launching Read to Someone by going over the I-chart. We review the sense of urgency for Read to Someone and the correct behaviors and look forward to tomorrow, when we will increase our practice time and build our stamina.

READ TO SOMEONE FOCUS LESSON DAY 2: I READ, YOU READ

We begin by reviewing yesterday's learning, asking students to turn to their elbow buddies and describe how their bodies look (EEKK) and what kind of voice we use while reading to someone. Then we launch into the day's lesson: "Today, before we practice again and work on building our stamina, I have a few more tricks to teach you about Read to Someone."

Directing their attention to a new anchor chart titled "Ways to Read to Someone" we say, "Yesterday when we read with our partners we had one person read while the other person held the check mark, listening and checking for understanding. When the partner was finished reading his or her section, you switched jobs. Today we're going to learn some other ways you might want to read books with your partner."

We explain that this second strategy is especially useful for improving fluency, and is called "I Read, You Read." "One of you will read a page or a paragraph, and then your partner will read the exact same page or paragraph, trying to make the reading sound just like yours. The person with the smoothest fluency should go first. Pat, can you help me model this for the class?" Pat joins me in front of the group. We sit down on the floor together. "What do you notice about how Pat and I are sitting together getting ready to read to each other?"

"You are sitting EEKK," says Mick.

"Good for you! Now let's watch as Pat and I model 'I Read, You Read.' Pat, who do you think should go first?"

"I think you should; you are way more fluent than I am."

So we begin reading the story (me aloud, and him silently following along). After the first page, Pat reads the same text, trying to make his pace and expression sound like mine. We follow the same procedure with the next page or paragraph. "Class, what do we call this type of reading?" They respond, "'I Read, You Read.'" We ask them to tell their elbow buddy how "I Read, You Read" helps them improve as readers, and listen as they identify fluency to each other.

We close the lesson with another option. "There is one more strategy I would like to show you so you have choices when you Read to Someone. It is called 'Read Two Different Books.'" We add "Read Two Different Books" to the anchor chart. "For this Read-to-Someone choice, you and your partner can both have different books, yet still read as partners. Here is how it goes. Malcom, will you help me model this one? You get a book from your book box, and I'll get a book from mine. What do you notice about our books?" (The book we pull from our teacher box is a long adult novel.)

Jolie: "Your book isn't a good-fit book for Malcom—it looks too hard."

"You are right! Malcom and I really want to read together, but my book is too hard for him. Even though my book is too hard for Malcom, we can still be partners and enjoy each other's books. Here's how. Malcom, you read the first page of your book to me. I'll keep my book closed with my finger marking my place. When you are finished reading the first page, I'll check for understanding. Then, you'll close your book, keeping your finger marking the page you're on, and you'll listen to me. When I am finished reading, you'll check for understanding and then we'll switch back again." We model together.

We then go back over and review three different ways to Read to Someone:

1. "Check for Understanding," one book: One partner reads while the other checks for understanding, then switch.
2. "I Read, You Read," one book: One partner reads; the other partner reads the same part of the story. The most fluent reader reads first.
3. "Read Two Different Books," two books: Partners read two different books and check for understanding.

Students are partnered up and placed around the room, the same as on Day One of Read to Someone. The difference is that today partners will decide together which of the three ways they will read. We will aim for one more minute than yesterday, building their stamina slowly so all students can be successful.

The process continues and ends the same as Day One with repeated modeling, practice, and checking in to build stamina.

READ-TO-SOMEONE FOCUS LESSON DAY 3: HOW TO CHOOSE BOOKS

We begin by reviewing the learning from the first two days of launching Read to Someone before moving into today's lesson. "Today we are going to learn some strategies for how to choose books. Put your thumbs up if you have ever had a friend over, decided to play a game, and couldn't agree on which one to play. You wanted to play one game, and your friend wanted to play a different one." Thumbs go up in the air and conversation erupts. All kids have some background knowledge about this problem!

"The same thing can happen with books when you choose to do Read to Someone. Today we want to teach you some strategies for how to choose books with your friends and classmates without getting into an argument." On the Read-to-Someone anchor chart under EEKK we write, "How to Choose Books."

"Lynn, would you like to help me model the first strategy? We call it 'Let's Make a Deal.' Lynn, would you get a book from your book box that you would like to read, and I'll get one from mine. Now pretend that we are partners and I tell you I *really* want us to read my book because it is my favorite! However, Lynn, you *really* want to read your book because it is *your* favorite." At this point we either move forward with the lesson as below, or spend some time having the kids brainstorm ideas that have worked for them to solve this problem.

"Here is how to solve this problem using 'Let's Make a Deal.' Hey, Lynn, how about if we read your book together first and then we read mine? Will that be okay with you?" Lynn agrees.

"Class, do you see how we made a deal? We quickly solved this problem so that we didn't waste any of our precious reading time disagreeing over which book to read. We could also have agreed to do Read Two Different Books. Another way to solve this problem would be to do Rock, Paper, Scissors, with the winner choosing the book this time." We add these ideas to the chart and then Lynn models with us, choosing which book to read by using Rock, Paper, Scissors.

READ-TO-SOMEONE FOCUS LESSON DAY 4: CHOOSING YOUR OWN CLASSROOM SPOT

After reviewing the I-chart for Read to Someone, we launch into the focus lesson on choosing your own spot to work in. "Each day as we have been practicing and building our stamina, I have been picking your partners for you and placing you around the room. You have experienced many good places to sit in our room. Today I will again pick your partners, but you and your partner will select a good place to read using what you know about good places for working."

Cheers go up in the room. We have been systematically teaching every behavior of Read to Self and Read to Someone, including where to sit. The correct modeling, incorrect modeling, and successful practice and reflection have trained the students' muscle memories, so this transition to more independence is smooth and part of the gradual release of responsibility. After we select their partners, they go by pairs to get their book boxes. Those of us in the gathering place watch and listen as the partners

- decide how they will do Read to Someone;
- move to a place in the room where they know they can be successful; and
- pick their books.

Continuing this a few partners at a time avoids a stampede and ensures a smooth and orderly start to our session.

After everyone has found a place to work, we build stamina by adding another minute or two to yesterday's time.

READ-TO-SOMEONE FOCUS LESSON DAY 5: HOW TO CHOOSE A PARTNER

After reviewing the I-chart for Read to Someone, we launch into today's lesson about choosing partners. "As we have been building our stamina each day and practicing all these parts of Read to Someone, I have been putting you into your partnerships. Today we will learn the correct way to pick a partner during Read to Someone or any time during our day." (We have prepared a blank anchor chart titled "How to Choose a Partner" ahead of time.) "When we choose partners, it is very important to remember that our partner doesn't always need to be our very closest friend. It is also great fun to read with other friends in our classroom. In fact, sometimes our very closest friends don't make the best partners, because we might have a tendency to chat instead of read." We write this first idea on our anchor chart—"Not always your closest friend."

"When it comes time to choose a partner, we want to communicate to the group that we need one, but what do you think would happen if we just started yelling, 'Hey, I need a partner!'" The class giggles. At this point in the year, they are becoming accustomed to the soft tone of our rooms, so the intrusion of our loud voices yelling for a partner is out of place and for some even a bit uncomfortable.

"Class, let's give that a try and see how it sounds. Okay, everyone, start yelling out to the rest of the class that you need a partner." Obviously, the sound is deafening. Some dramatically put their hands over their ears; others laugh at this absurdity. "That will never work in our classroom, will it? There has to be another way to communicate our need for a partner."

We either ask for ideas from the group—how do you think kids in our room could communicate the need for a partner—or we guide this part of the lesson as below.

"Here is a great, quiet way to let people know we need a partner." (We add these to the anchor chart as we say and model them.)

1. Close your mouth and raise your hand. This is our class's silent signal that will mean "I need a partner." (Model for class.)
2. Look around the group. When you see another person with a hand raised, make eye contact with him or her. (Model for class.)
3. Walk *to* the person and say, "Will you please be my partner?" We model this part of the lesson because we are very particular about tone of voice. We model asking it with an inviting tone. The only acceptable answer is "Sure, thank you!" Again, we model the tone we expect to hear during the response, pleased and polite.

"The tone of voice is very important in our classroom. How would you like it if someone came up to you and used the correct words, 'Will you please be my partner?' but said it flatly, and kind of grumpily? Madeline, will you help me model this? I am going to ask you to be my partner with a crummy, grumpy tone of voice, and let's have you tell us how it feels." We proceed to model the wrong way and ask Madeline, "How did it feel?"

Madeline replies, "I didn't think you really wanted to be my partner. I didn't like it at all."

"Madeline, now let's model for the class using the right tone of voice." We model for the class using the correct tone of voice, really emphasizing the end of the sentence.

"Well, Madeline, what did you think that time?"

"I thought you were really excited about being my partner and I couldn't wait to read with you, too!"

"Boys and girls, that is exactly how we want our partners to feel, like we are really excited to read with them, because then, they will be excited about reading with us! Who else would like to model for us?" We are very purposeful about giving every child in the class a chance to model putting his or her hand up, making eye contact, walking to a partner, asking to be partners, and responding with a nice tone of voice. This can be challenging for our shy students, and we watch them closely for a few days to see if they need support. After they have a few positive interactions, with our coaching and support on the side, they are ready to do it on their own. We continue to practice for a few minutes, making certain that every child has had numerous chances to visually see how to choose a partner, hear what it sounds like, and kinesthetically practice. This practice helps secure the behaviors into their muscle memories and into their default behavior.

READ-TO-SOMEONE FOCUS LESSON DAY 6:
COACHING OR TIME?

After reviewing the previous day's learning and charts, we begin by asking, "How many of you play a sport like soccer, baseball, basketball, or any others? Which person helps you know what to do while you are playing?"

The class chimes in with "The coach!"

"Yes, a coach is a person who can give you help when you need it, tells you 'you can do it,' and gives you support. Today we are going to learn a bit about being a reading coach. Put your thumb up if you have ever been reading with a partner and come to a word you didn't know."

Sierra, a reluctant reader in our classroom, says, "Sometimes the partner just says the word for me, even though I was trying to figure it out on my own."

"Have any of the rest of you had that same thing happen?" Heads nod enthusiastically. "How many of you wish that your partner would give you a chance to try to figure it out on your own using your strategies?" Again, a round of nods.

"But sometimes when I am really stuck on a word, I like it when my partner helps me," offers Emily.

"Good point, Emily. The trick is to know when someone wants help or wants to do it alone. Think about when you are playing a sport such as baseball. There are times when the coach will come up behind you and really help you, showing you how to hold the bat and swing at the ball. Other times, the coach may just encourage you, not stepping in to help you at all. It is very similar in reading. At times when you can't remember what you read or get stuck on a word, you want someone to give you ideas and suggestions, just like the batting coach. There are other times when you want to try it on your own. Good reading coaches don't just step in and tell their partners the words right away. That doesn't help them become better readers!

"Here is what it looks like to be a good reading coach." We begin a new chart with the title "Reading Coach" on the top.

"When your partner comes to a word he or she doesn't know, or he or she can't remember or understand what the story was about, you are going to count to three silently to yourself." On the chart we write "Silently count to three."

"After you silently count to three, ask your partner, "Do you want coaching or time?" On the chart we write "Ask, coaching or time?"

"If your partner says, 'Time,' you must sit patiently and wait. If your partner says, 'Coaching,' you will take out your coaching sheet [see Figure 5-6] and decide which strategy would be best to suggest." We add to the chart, "Use coaching sheet."

"Let's practice. Ben, would you like to model?" We take the coaching sheet and ask Ben to get a book from his book box, read a bit, and then find a word that he either doesn't know or can pretend not to know. When he comes to the word he doesn't know, we go through the coaching steps, using metacognition to show the rest of the class what we would do with Ben.

"Oh, Ben is stuck on a word. I'll count silently to three to give him some time to figure it out." We count silently, but put our fingers up one at a time. After the count of a very slow three (about one count every two seconds), we ask softly, "Ben, would you like time or coaching?" Ben says, "Time." Again through the metacognitive process we let them know what we are thinking. "Ah, Ben wants time to figure this word out, so I am going to sit patiently and look at the word and think about what coaching strategy will work best if he changes his mind." We then model sitting patiently until Ben says the word.

We now ask Ben if he will read a bit more, this time coming to a word he doesn't know and asking for coaching. He begins reading and gets stuck. We think aloud to show the children what is going on in our brains. "Hmmm, Ben is stuck on this word. I remember that I am supposed to count to three to give him time to figure it out." Again, we model counting silently, putting up three fingers one at a time to indicate our counting to three. At the end of three we ask Ben, "Would you like time or coaching?"

This time Ben asks for coaching. We take out our coaching sheet and model looking over the sheet and picking a strategy that might help him.

"Ben, have you tried 'Back Up and Reread'?" He says he has but it didn't work. "Okay, how about 'Chunk Sounds Together'?" Ben tries chunking the word, gets the word, and keeps reading. We point out to the class that we did not tell Ben the word; instead we gave him ideas of which strategy might help him figure it out.

Each of the strategies is taught individually and added to the coaching sheet afterward. As the year progresses and the strategies become intuitive, the need to refer to the coaching sheet is unnecessary.

Figure 5-6 Coaching Sheet

Reading Words
■ What strategy have you used?
■ Go back and reread.
■ Skip the word and come back.
■ Chunk sounds together.
■ What word could fit here?
■ Look at the pictures—the word is right here.
■ I am going to sound this word out with you.
■ I am going to tell you the word.

Comprehension
■ I will retell what has happened so far.
■ Fill in the who, what, where, and why.
■ Would it help if I summarized the story for you?

After modeling for the children, it is time to move into the correct model/incorrect model phase of the lesson. The rest of this lesson continues in the same format, increasing students' stamina.

LISTEN TO READING

It was amazing for us to see students develop such language fluency from reading books with audiotapes that they were able to wean themselves from the recordings. We watched them use the tapes for support as they chose increasingly difficult texts, thereby compensating for the difference between their listening and reading vocabularies.

—*Janet Allen,* **Yellow Brick Roads: Shared and Guided Paths to Independent Reading 4–12**

Children come to us with varying backgrounds and levels of family support. We have found it necessary to provide the "lap time" that many of our children have missed out on. Parent and grandparent volunteers and older reading buddies may help fill this deficit for children who have missed the auditory support of being read to. Books on tape, CD, or computer are also valuable resources. These audio stories are also helpful supports for our students who get their first exposure to English when they enter our classrooms. So during the Daily Five, children may choose Listen to Reading instead of partner reading or Read to Self on a particular day.

Figure 5-7 Listen to Reading

Keeping headphones in working order has been difficult for us. We also remember the lice epidemic one year when we had to bag all the headphones for two weeks. The solution came when we discovered that teachers could put small headphones on school supply lists. These can be purchased for a few dollars. Children bring them to school, write their names on their headphones with a small piece of tape, and wrap the tape around the headphones. They are stored in a small zippered plastic bag and housed in each child's book box. The headsets are ready at a moment's notice for each child, whether they are working on Listen to Reading or quietly using the computer.

Many teachers have found great success without using headphones, instead teaching the children an appropriate volume for the tape player, allowing more children to listen to the story at one time.

Figure 5-8 Listen to Reading I-Chart

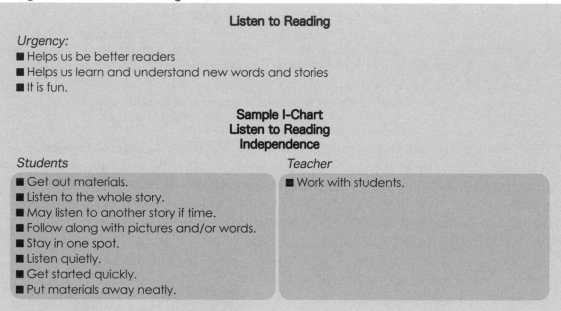

Listen to Reading

Urgency:
■ Helps us be better readers
■ Helps us learn and understand new words and stories
■ It is fun.

Sample I-Chart
Listen to Reading
Independence

Students	*Teacher*
■ Get out materials.	■ Work with students.
■ Listen to the whole story.	
■ May listen to another story if time.	
■ Follow along with pictures and/or words.	
■ Stay in one spot.	
■ Listen quietly.	
■ Get started quickly.	
■ Put materials away neatly.	

We launch Listen to Reading with a discussion. "Today we will add our next Daily Five by learning how to be independent with Listen to Reading. Let's begin by talking about why we would listen to reading."

Amy: "I guess it is to help us be better readers, because look at all the others [pointing to the other four I-charts in our gathering place]. They all help us with that."
Lori: "I know one: it is fun! My mom and I check out books on tape from the library all the time, and we listen to the stories. I love to do that. It's really fun!"

It is not uncommon for children to connect the ideas from each of the Daily Five together like Amy and Lori, because they all follow the same pattern of introduction. This is one of the great advantages to a consistent, explicit instructional pattern when introducing anything new.

Many of the kids will not come up with the idea that listening to reading helps us understand new words and stories; this is one that we usually tell them about.

FOCUS LESSONS

The focus lessons for Listen to Reading are simple and direct. We start with talk among friends. "Boys and girls, we listen to reading often each day. Turn to your elbow buddy and talk to them about the times during the day that you might listen to reading." They will come up with shared reading, teacher read aloud, Read to Someone, sometimes guided reading, and possibly when an adult reads to them at home.

"Today, we are going to add another type of listening to reading to the Daily Five. We are going to add listening to a book on tape." We follow the lesson below whether our classroom is equipped with tapes, CDs, or a computer.

"In our classroom we have four small tape players with headphones, along with a basket of books. You can choose these tape players as one of the ways to listen to stories in school. Let me show you how to set up the tape player and follow along with the book." This part of the lesson will vary, depending on the type of machine you will be using. It is important to show the class how to use the machine without your help so they can be independent.

Figure 5-9 Focus Lessons for Listen to Reading

Day 1
■ Brainstorm I-chart of expected behaviors.
■ Model and practice material setup of tape/CD recorder, book, and using recorder.
■ Model and practice listening and following along with words and/or pictures.

Day 2
■ Review I-chart.
■ Model and practice putting materials away neatly.

Day 3
■ Review I-chart.
■ Model and practice listening to a short story, finishing it, and starting a new story.
■ Model and practice what to do if work time is up before the story is finished.

Day 4
■ Review I-chart.
■ Discuss the number of recorders available.
■ Decide on a way that allows all to participate. (Eventually many children will lose interest and you can nudge those who will truly benefit.)
■ See "check-in" in Chapter 3 for ideas on who listens first, second, and so on.

Often we watch the class as they use the equipment and see which ones have had some experience with tape players, computers, CDs, and so on. They will then become the "Listen-to-Reading helpers" so that kids who are having difficulty will go to them rather than to us. As time goes on, all kids become proficient at using the Listen-to-Reading tools.

"It's time to make our I-chart for Listen to Reading. Let's brainstorm together the behaviors that someone who chooses to listen to reading would need to have to be independent." Most of the behaviors you want on the I-chart are similar to or the same as ones the class will have experienced with the introduction of other components of the Daily Five. Those behaviors that the children do not come up with, we suggest.

"Just like we have done before, let's see if there is someone who can model the right way." The student models getting the tape player, choosing a book and tape, and finding a quiet place in the room to listen.

"Now that we've seen Listen to Reading modeled the right way, who would like to model the wrong way?" By this point in the introduction, you may have many students who want to model the wrong way. We stick with choosing a student whom we anticipate will be challenged by Listen to Reading. He or she shows the class the wrong behaviors and then models it correctly.

This is one area of Daily Five instruction that varies a bit from the other four. Obviously, we cannot have the whole class practice Listen to Reading at once. Therefore, we have the same number of children practice as we have tape players, while the other children are working on the other components of the Daily Five. We've found that there is very little need to build stamina here. Listening to reading is so engaging for children that most have no problem sticking with it for an extended period of time.

06

WORK ON WRITING AND WORD WORK

■■■□□

In helping students tune their ears—and mouths and eyes, even their fingertips, their nerve endings—to the glorious range of ways they can string words together, we need to encourage them to fool around, to experiment, to break rules even before they know all the rules. Who ever knows *all* the rules, anyway?

—*Judith Rowe Michaels*

■■■□□

Intensive work (and play) in writing and word study also supports reading development. The two components of the Daily Five, Work on Writing and Word Work, help students hone their skills as writers and their knowledge of words. By now, many students are becoming comfortable with the gradual-release model used to launch the Daily Five elements. They anticipate and receive plenty of modeling, repeated practice, and lessons designed to help them understand expectations.

The writing component of the Daily Five provides additional support children require to become effective writers. Its purpose is to provide daily writing practice and intense focused instruction via one-on-one conferences, small guided writing groups, and whole-group focus lessons. We use it as a twenty- to thirty-minute supplement to writer's workshop, which takes place each afternoon in our classrooms. We have seen a direct correlation between student motivation, ability, and productivity and this increase in writing practice. It goes back to purpose. Kids who have a purpose care about their writing and the people who will read it.

WORK ON WRITING

During the Work on Writing session, students work individually or with a partner on writing of their choice. As Ralph Fletcher says, "You don't learn to write by going through a series of preset writing exercises. You learn to write by grappling with a real subject that truly matters to you." Working on writing provides students with time to spend on writing that really matters to them:

- Persuasive writing, convincing friends to read a favorite book
- Friendly letters to a classmate or pen pal
- Recount of a lost tooth or the loss of a beloved pet
- Reports on topics of current interest
- Poetry
- Narrative about a sport game

Typically children use Work-on-Writing time to continue the work they have been doing during writer's workshop. The main difference between the two is that during the workshop, we may ask students to produce a piece of writing based on a strategy or genre being taught, but during the Daily Five it is sustained writing of their choice.

LAUNCHING WORK ON WRITING

We begin, as always, by setting a purpose for this element of the Daily Five. "Today we are going to begin our very first day of the Daily Five's Work on Writing. We will be doing Work on Writing every day. Turn to an elbow buddy and talk over why you think it is so important to write every day." By the time we introduce Work on Writing to the class, we are quite confident that the majority of students will be able to come up with one or two reasons it is so important to write each day.

Figure 6-1 Work-on-Writing I-Chart

Work on Writing

Urgency:
- Helps us become better readers and writers
- We care about writing and the people who read it.
- Choice
- It is fun.
- Works on the fluency of writing

Sample I-Chart
Work on Writing
Independence

Students	*Teacher*
■ Write the whole time.	■ Work with students.
■ Stay in one spot.	
■ Work quietly.	
■ Choice of what to write.	
■ Get started quickly.	
■ Underline words we're not sure how to spell and move on.	

"Who would like to share your partner's ideas of why it is so important to write every day?"

Scott: "Emily said because it is the best way to become a better writer." As Scott says this, he glances at the I-chart for Read to Self that is hanging in our gathering place. He has made the connection between the sense of urgency for Read to Self and Work on Writing.
Jolie: "I think we write every day because it is fun!" (Jolie thinks *everything* is fun!)

We keep taking ideas from the children. Often children are unaware of the idea "We care about our writing and the people who read it." Or that just as with Read to Self and Read to Someone, they get to choose what they want to write. If neither of these ideas comes up with the students, we'll add them to the list.

FOCUS LESSONS

At this time, we get ready to do a modeled writing lesson showing the class what to do when faced with a word they can't spell. We have found this focus lesson to be a crucial step in creating independent writers who can sustain writing for extended periods of time. It is an expectation we will continue to model throughout the year, regardless of the focus-lesson topic. "Friends, before we brainstorm what independent writers do in our classroom, there is something you need to know that will really help you with your independence." With a marker and blank piece of paper, we turn to the chart rack and think aloud before we begin our story.

"Let's pretend this is my writer's notebook. I will use this chart paper instead of my notebook so you can all see what I think about when writing. Last night the weirdest thing happened, and I just couldn't wait to write about it in my writer's notebook. I was sitting outside after dinner reading a book when I heard the rush of wings right above my head. I looked up from my book to see a huge owl land on the railing of my deck. I sat perfectly still, hardly daring to breathe. The owl was staring very intently into the grassy area below. Suddenly the owl seemed to fall right off the edge of the deck! I jumped up and ran to the deck's edge just in time to see the owl grab a huge rat and take off flying with it into the air. What a good dinner for the owl!

"Okay, there is my plan for what I will write about. Now I am ready to get started." With that, we pick up the marker, and, starting from the beginning of the story, write the words, modeling very explicitly how to write the sounds we hear in words or sight words we have memorized. After writing the first three words, we pause. "Boys and girls, I don't know how to spell *weirdest,* but I really want to use that word. When writers in our room come to a word they don't know how to spell, they just write the sounds they hear, put a line under it so they can come back to it later, then keep writing." We write the following on the chart paper:

"Last night the *weerdest* thing happened to me . . ."

"Did you notice that I did not get up to ask anyone how to spell the word? I will work on the correct spelling later."

We continue writing in front of the class for just another sentence or so, modeling a couple more times how we underline words we don't know, then keep going.

Figure 6-2 Focus Lessons for Work on Writing

Day 1
- ■ Model what to do when writing words they can't spell. (Underline and go on.)
- ■ Brainstorm I-chart.

Day 2
- ■ Brainstorm and practice where to sit.
- ■ Brainstorm and practice what materials to use during writing.
  - ■ Notebook
  - ■ Pencil or pen
  - ■ Drawing or sketching

Day 3
- ■ What to write about . . .
  - ■ Make a list of topics (vacation, dog, sister, etc.).
  - ■ Make a list of forms (letters, lists, narrative).
  - ■ Post lists for students' reference.

Day 4 +
- ■ Continue to teach the forms and traits of writing according to your district curriculum.

Once a focus lesson is taught, students work on writing—building stamina.

Add a few minutes each day until primary students are up to 30 minutes and intermediate students can sustain for 45 minutes.

Next, we brainstorm with students the behaviors for writing independently.

Because this activity has been done with other Daily Five components, students have a good idea of what it will look and sound like. They quickly volunteer behaviors independent writers will use and we write them on the I-chart. If students do not volunteer some of the ideas we want (see sample I-chart), we elicit the ideas by reviewing the Read-to-Self and Read-to-Someone charts, or share the desired behaviors ourselves. It is exciting to hear children chime right in when filling out the teacher side of the I-chart. They understand that we will be actively engaged with teaching children individually or in small groups.

"Friends, now let's see if anyone in our room would like to model Work on Writing the correct way for us." We have one to three students take turns getting their book boxes, which have their writer's notebooks in them, move to a quiet place, and model writing independently in front of the whole class.

"Who would like to model the wrong way for us?" We pick someone we suspect will have difficulty staying engaged in Work on Writing.

"Now we are going to have a three-minute practice." Groans from the group are usually heard now. They are already building such stamina during Read to Self and Read

Figure 6-3 a and b Students write around the room.

to Someone that most of the class knows how to sustain for longer than three minutes. For the first few days, we place children with their book boxes (which contain their writer's notebooks and a pen or pencil) around the room, showing them all the different places a writer may sit.

Once everyone has a place to sit, we move out of their way, not making eye contact or putting anyone back on-task. Often their stamina has developed enough from Read to Self that they are able to write for longer than three minutes. However, as soon as one child goes off-task, we give the signal to regroup at the gathering place for check-in, reviewing the anchor chart.

WORD WORK

Creating and maintaining a time during each literacy block to focus on words is critical to developing readers, writers, and communicators. Word study takes up a portion of our literacy block, allowing time for the following:

- ■ Experimenting with words for learning and practicing a spelling pattern
- ■ Memorizing high-frequency words
- ■ Generalizing spelling patterns
- ■ Adding to our knowledge and curiosity of unique and interesting words

During Word Work we focus on spelling and vocabulary work with children. There is considerable controversy about the best way to teach these. The Daily Five structure does not dictate the best method to use in teaching reading, writing, spelling, or vocabulary work, but instead creates a richly literate environment that provides essential and often-skipped practice time. Whatever your preferred method of instruction, it can take place in a daily Word Work focus lesson.

LAUNCHING WORD WORK

By the time we reach the last component of the Daily Five, students are comfortable with and accomplished at following routines. "Today we are going to learn the procedures for how to use our spelling materials. We are going to learn how to set them up, how to use them, and how to clean them up. It is important to spell words correctly when we write, because we care about our writing and the people who will read it. Spending time practicing spelling helps us become not only better spellers and writers, but also better readers. Do you know what else? It is fun!"

Figure 6–4 Word-Work I-Charts for Materials

**Word Work
Spelling and Vocabulary**

Urgency:
■ It helps us become better readers, writers, and spellers.
■ We care about our writing and the people who will read it.
■ It is fun.

**Sample I-Chart for
Word Work
Materials Setup
Independence**

Students

■ One person takes out materials of his or her choice and sets up in a quiet location.
■ Stay in one spot until time to return materials.
■ Work the whole time.
■ Try your best.
■ Work on stamina.
■ Work quietly.
■ Get started quickly.

Teacher

■ Work with students.

Optional Material Ideas:
■ Whiteboards
■ Magnetic letters
■ Wikki Stix
■ Clay
■ Letter stamps
■ Colored markers

**Sample I-Chart for
Word Work
How to Use Materials
Independence**

Students

■ Work the whole time.
■ Stay in one spot except to get and return materials.
■ May return one set of materials and get another set to work with.
■ Work quietly.
■ Work on stamina.
■ Try your best.
■ Get started quickly.

Teacher

■ Work with students.

"Let's begin by writing down a list of some of the materials we can use to practice spelling."
We write the following:

- Whiteboards
- Magnetic letters
- Wikki Stix
- Clay
- Letter stamps
- Colored markers

"Now let's make an I-chart with our ideas about ways to set up the materials and how to explore and use them."

We explain that we are going to talk about what it looks like, sounds like, and feels like to be independent during Word Work setup, including working with the materials and what the teacher is doing.

Jenna: "I know what the teacher does—you are working with kids. This is just like Read to Self! We have to be independent so we can get better at spelling, and you can help teach us."
"Wow, Jenna, you are such a wise thinker to remember that this is following the same Daily Five pattern." (We write Jenna's idea down, with her name beside it.)
Zoe: "I think when we set the materials up, we have to make good choices where we sit, just like in Read to Self."
Zoe turns to Jenna grinning, clearly pleased that she, too, is a wise thinker.
"Ahh, Zoe found another way this is similar to Read to Self!"
Hermando: "When we work with the spelling stuff, we should work quietly."
Kelsey: "I really think we should try our best."
We add all these ideas to the chart, with the children's names beside them.

Each year, we wonder if our children will come up with these ideas. Then we remember that they have a lot of previous Daily Five experience to draw from. It is our job to help tie the Daily Five together for the children. If we do a good job of introducing the first Daily, learning the subsequent Daily Five components happens more quickly, and the muscle memory is deeper.

The children continue offering suggestions for setting up and working with materials, and these are recorded on the chart. Here are some of the suggestions that you will want to be certain are included:

- One person takes out the materials of his or her choice and sets them up in a quiet location.
- Get started quickly.
- Stay in one spot except to get and return the materials.
- Work the whole time.
- Work quietly.
- Work on stamina.
- Try your best.

We direct students to the location of the materials, which we usually keep in one central place. They are clearly marked and labeled with words and pictures on both the tub and the shelf. This assures that children can be completely independent with material setup and cleanup. We don't have to waste a minute of our teaching time doing things that our children are capable of doing once they are taught how.

"Who would like to model setting up the materials using the ideas we came up with on our I-chart?" Hands fly in the air. We choose one student per spelling material to model the setup of materials correctly.

"Now who would like to model this incorrectly?"

Once again, hands wave frantically in the air. We are very particular about whom we choose. By this time we have a general idea of who might not find this type of activity successful and who might need some extra preparation. We choose a student we suspect will find this challenging. Remember, give that student an audience now, or he or she will certainly take it later! Have the student model the setup incorrectly. Once he or she has received attention for this inappropriate behavior, have the student turn right around and set the materials up the correct way so you and everyone can watch.

Figure 6-5 Independent Word Work

Once materials are set up, we begin placing children around the room near the spelling materials. Children practice and explore working with the materials according to the chart. We know that unless children have ample time to explore and play with the materials, they will be unable to use them as tools for spelling practice. Therefore over the course of the next four days or so, children will have plenty of time to explore the variety of materials as they build their stamina for doing Word Work.

After three to five minutes we signal students to gather and check in on how setup and working with the materials went. We make any necessary additions to the I-chart.

"We have had one practice time. Don't worry—we will have lots of time this week and all year long to work with these materials. Right now we need to spend some time talking about a very important part of our Word Work time: cleanup!

"You are learning the correct ways to get the materials out independently. You are also learning how to work independently with the materials. Now we need to learn how to put the materials away independently, so they are ready for the next person.

"Let's start another I-chart and label it 'Word Work—Material Cleanup Independence.' Who has some ideas of how students in our room who are independent will clean up the materials?" At this point, suggestions are taken and written on the chart, as described. Someone will add the idea that the teacher is working with students. We want to constantly reinforce the message that children are independent so they can get to be better readers and writers, but also that the teacher has a very important job to do—teach children.

Figure 6-6 Focus Lessons for Word Work

Day 1
- Introduce optional materials and their locations to students.
- Brainstorm I-chart(s) of how to set up materials and how to work with them independently. (See sample I-charts for materials setup and use.)
- Model finding the materials, materials placement in the room, and setup of materials.
- Brainstorm chart of how to clean up. (See sample I-chart of How to Clean Up, below.)
- Model materials placement in the room, setup and cleanup of the materials.

Day 2
- Model and practice materials setup, materials placement, and cleanup of materials.
- Brainstorm I-chart—"How to Use Materials."
- Model and practice student behaviors of how to use materials.
- Continue building stamina of working with materials, adding one to two minutes each day.

Other focus lessons for Word Work might include the following:
- Word sorts
- Adding words to their collection
- Add words in their word study notebooks that relate to the strategy taught that day, e.g., long words, or blends that have *ck, nd, ng,* or *nk*.
- Practicing basic words most often misspelled
- Open word sort and write words in word-study notebook.
- Closed word sort and write words in word-study notebook.
- List words that belong to a pattern and add to notebook.
- Set up notebook.

Each day add a few more minutes until students are independently working with these materials for up to 30 minutes for primary students and 45 minutes for intermediate students.

Here are some of the ideas that we find necessary to have on the chart:

- Clean quietly.
- Everyone who was using the materials helps put them away.
- Materials go back in their tub, and the tub goes back to the same spot on the shelf.
- Leave the materials neat—it's respectful to our friends in our classroom.
- Get started on your new task quickly.

"Okay, who would like to model how to put the materials away for us?" Two or three students model putting the materials away according to the chart. Once again, one or two carefully chosen students model it the wrong way and then the right way.

We bring students back to the gathering spot and check in. At this time, all materials are put away, allowing us flexibility in repeating the practice or waiting until tomorrow.

By the time our students have mastered Word Work, they have mastered the Daily Five. They now know everything they need to know about where materials are in the classroom, how we expect them to work independently and with peers, and how to organize and monitor their time. Perhaps most important, this thoughtful, sustained independent work in literacy has become a daily habit for them.

Figure 6-7 Word Work—Material Cleanup Independence I-Chart

Sample I-Chart
Word Work
Material Cleanup
Independence

Students	Teacher
■ Everyone using materials helps put those materials away. ■ Materials go back in the original tub. ■ Return materials to the same spot. ■ Leave the materials neat. ■ Clean quietly. ■ Get started on your new task quickly.	■ Work with students.

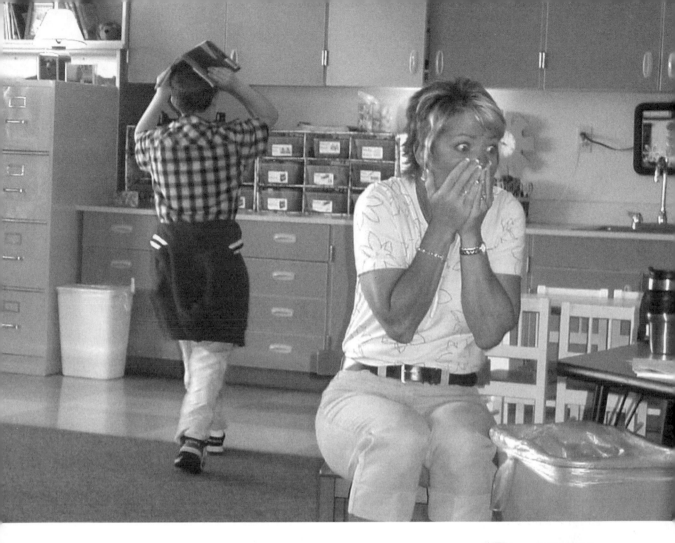

07

PUTTING IT ALL TOGETHER AND TROUBLESHOOTING

■■■□□

Each problem that I solved became a rule which served afterwards to solve other problems.

—Rene Descartes

■■■□□

During the first month of school, as we are launching each component of Daily Five, we feel somewhat like jugglers spinning plates. We start spinning the first plate of Read to Self. It wobbles a bit, but with a few flicks of our wrists it is soon spinning on its own. That's when we add the next component of the Daily Five. Once it is spinning, we introduce another. As each new plate is added to our juggling act, it takes a mere flick of the wrist to keep all five plates balanced in the air, working together, finely tuned.

By October, all children are able to work independently in unison on each Daily Five choice for at least twelve to twenty minutes. The total time for independent literacy work now ranges from sixty to a hundred minutes.

The phone call between the two of us in October is always the same.

"Are your students ready for the next step of Daily Five?"

"You mean, are they ready to decide the order in which they will carry out the Daily Five components?"

"What if this class hasn't practiced the behaviors enough to transfer them throughout the literacy block?"

"What about Travis? I am worried that this could undo all the progress he has made sustaining independence with each of the Daily Five components."

"It is going so well having them all participate in Read to Self at the same time, then Read to Someone at the same time, Work on Writing at the same time, and Word Work at the same time, why would I want to mess with a good thing?"

"Will they be able manage their behaviors as well when all five choices are going on simultaneously?"

We know and believe in our heart of hearts that children become more engaged, motivated, and successful when they have choice over what they read, what they write, and the order in which they schedule their days. Nevertheless we have found it hard to give up being in control of their literacy choices.

Then we think about our own need for choice. We realize we have much in common with our children. There are days when we come to school ready to settle in and get right down to business. Other days, working alone doesn't seem as enticing, so we collaborate with our teaching partners. Our needs tend to dictate how we organize our time and activities. If a quiet morning of preparation is interrupted by a staff meeting, our minds and bodies resist.

We are more motivated, engaged, and productive when we are in control of our schedules. We know the expectations of our jobs and want to be trusted to choose the order of our daily schedules and the approaches we take to meeting them. Why should our children feel any differently? This, we believe, is at the heart of choice: knowing the expectations, possessing the skills to meet them, being trusted to carry them out, and taking responsibility to do so. It is what we desire and provide for our students. With this aspiration in mind our phone call ends with,

"If you kick off total choice tomorrow, so will I!"

"Our kids can do it."

"Let's check in at lunch."

So, remembering our promise to each other, we begin the next day's focus lesson by introducing choice.

"Boys and girls, we are so excited about our day today. You have learned how to be independent throughout the Daily Five. This is one of the most exciting days of all. Today you will be completely in charge of the order in which you do each of the Daily Five. Some of you may choose Read to Self first, others may choose to Read to Someone, Work on Writing, Word Work, or even Listen to Reading. You all know why you are doing each choice and how to be working independently. We trust you to be independent during the time you work on your Daily Five choice just like you have learned and practiced."

Dan, with his eyes sparkling, says, "You mean you aren't going to tell us what to do?"

"No," we respond. "We trust you to make a choice that feels right to your brain and body. Dan, what do you feel like starting with today?"

"Yesterday I was writing a story about scoring a goal in my soccer game; I wanted to finish it then but didn't have time. Could I finish it now?"

"Absolutely," we say. "Class, take a few moments, close your eyes, and think about which Daily you would like to begin with. Make a picture in your mind of what your body looks like, sounds like, and feels like while you're engaged in that choice."

At this time, we grab our "check-in" page. (See Figure 7-1.) Calling each child's name, we ask them to tell us what their first Daily Five choice will be.

CHECK IN

Students answer the question "What are you doing today?" Atwell calls this the "status-of-the-class conference" (1987, p. 89) and explains that taking three minutes to poll children about what each is doing that day creates immediate focus for the child's work and is time well spent. Every session, each student's response is recorded on a form like the one in Figure 7-1.

When Dan says, "Work on Writing," we place a *W* in the first box beside his name. When Michelle says, "Read to Self," we place an *R* in the first box next to her name. Emily tells us that her first choice today will be Word Work; *WW* is placed by her name. Diana wants to read to someone, so she has an *RS* placed by her name. We continue to go through the checklist, calling out each child's name, marking down their choices while they all remain at the gathering place. When children verbalize their choices, there is a sense of increased accountability. They take the choice very seriously, get started right away, and stick with it.

Figure 7-1 Check-in Page

	Monday					Tuesday					Wednesday				
Ben	R	RS	W	WW	L										
Kayla	RS	WW	W	L	R										
Madeline	W	L	RS	W	R										
Scott	R	W	WW	RS	L										
Jolie	R	RS	L	WW	W										
Mathew	WW	RS	W	L	R										
Emily	L	R	RS	WW	W										
Dan	RS	R	L	W	WW										
Jenna	W	WW	L	RS	R										
Hailey	R	RS	WW	W	L										
Peter	W	R	RS	WW	L										
Mick	R	RS	W	WW	L										
Kelsey	RS	WW	W	L	R										
Zoe	W	L	RS	W	R										
Dean	W	L	RS	W	R										
Karyn	R	RS	L	WW	W										
Lynn	RS	WW	W	L	R										
Jim	W	L	RS	W	R										
Michelle	RS	R	L	W	WW										
Diana	W	WW	L	RS	R										
Doug	L	RS	R	WW	W										
Marilyn	RS	W	WW	R	L										

R: Read to Self   WW: Word Work   RS: Read to Someone
L: Listen to Reading   W: Work on Writing

Once everyone has checked in, and before we release them to begin, we count how many students plan to do Read to Someone.

"Class, we have seven people who would like to do Read to Someone."

"Hey, that's an odd number!" calls out Guy. He and the rest of the class know that we do Read to Someone only in groups of two, as we have found two to be the optimum number. We have Guy do a quick account of how he knew it was an odd number (we never have to teach odd numbers in the math program again!), then ask, "What do you think we should do about this? Can anyone help us out?" There are always one or two children in the Read-to-

Someone group who offer to make a different choice for now and do Read-to-Someone next time, or someone else switches into Read to Someone, making it an even number.

Next we ask, "Would each of you close your eyes again and make a picture in your mind, seeing yourself independently doing your choice? Okay, here we go. If you are doing Listen to Reading, get up, get your supplies, find a place in the room where you can listen to reading independently, and get started."

As they get up and move, the rest of the class sits quietly, waiting until the Listen-to-Reading group is settled. "Now, those who are reading to yourselves go get your book boxes, find a place in the room where you can work independently, and get started." The rest of the group waits for those reading to themselves to find their places. "Next those working on writing go get your book boxes, get set up, and get started." Again, the remainder of the class waits. "Next, Word-Work group, please get your materials, set up, and get started working independently." Those who remain in the gathering place are the children who checked in to Read to Someone. "Finally, those reading to someone, find a partner and your book boxes, get set up, and get started.

"If you are reading to someone, please remember to check the area around you for friends who are reading to themselves or working on writing before you set up. You will want to respect their learning by not sitting too close to them."

We discover that it is best when groups leave the gathering place one at a time. This helps avoid the "stampede effect." Releasing them in small groups sets the tone for a calm and productive work time.

We look around, hardly able to believe our eyes. The children are independently working on all components of the Daily Five. There is the lovely hum to the room that signifies engaged ownership of learning. It is absolutely magical! We can now gather a small group for a guided lesson or confer with children one at a time without fear of interruption.

Figure 7-2 Students work independently on Word Work and Read to Self.

We have achieved what we set out to accomplish when we began this journey: providing children with meaningful literacy activities that will help them become proficient, lifelong learners while allowing us to work with small groups or individuals.

Our lunchtime check-in is always the same. "How did it go for you?"

"Amazing! How about for you?"

"Magic!"

TROUBLESHOOTING

We designed this book to help teachers successfully launch the Daily Five. One of our fears is that teachers will get the impression that the Daily Five focus lessons always revolve around management behaviors. This couldn't be further from our intent or our teaching practice.

By mid-October, very little, if any, of our instructional time each day is spent on management issues. Our students know what is expected, they thoroughly enjoy the choice and responsibility inherent in the Daily Five structure, and they move easily from working independently on the Daily Five tasks to small-group and whole-class lessons. Therefore, after the launching phase, the Daily Five focus lessons cease to be about behaviors of independence and instead address everything from how themes work in children's literature, to crafting a compelling lead in writing, to tackling blends and digraphs while reading. On any given day, there will be four or five thirty-minute independent work sessions, broken up by whole-class focus lessons, small-group and one-on-one teaching, and meeting instructional needs that have been determined by both formal and informal assessments.

We have worked with thousands of teachers over the past six years to help them implement the Daily Five, and some of our deepest reflections have come from the questions they ask. Many of their questions have challenged us, helping us tease out what ingrained habits we have that ensure the success of the Daily Five. For most of the questions there is no one answer. We understand that every classroom is unique, and the answers can be as varied as the people who ask and the children they are working with. We have reserved this last section of the book to address the thoughtful questions that many of you have asked us over the years.

My schedule is so odd—some days music, gym, and other special subjects break the day into small chunks; other days have no interruptions at all. How do I establish the Daily Five routines when my daily schedule varies so much?

Some years teachers happen to get "the schedule" that is chopped up by recess, lunch, and specialist work. We have experienced this ourselves! You may find yourself with very small chunks of instructional time. Then there are the schedules that contain a block of two or two-and-a-half hours for literacy. Both schedules have advantages and disadvantages. We have found Daily Five to be flexible enough to accommodate the year-to-year changes in our schedules.

The years we have had schedules containing those two-and-a-half-hour blocks, we have worried that the time is too long to keep kids engaged and focused. However, the children have been so well prepared to be independent, and the structure of Daily Five has so much movement interspersed with focused work time and instruction, that even little children could easily manage two-and-a-half hours straight with no recess.

In other years when our blocks of time were interrupted by everything from recess, to PE, to assemblies, to music, Daily Five worked just as well. The success lies in the explanation of the schedule to the children.

Our colleague Lori's Daily Five schedule was split by lunch. She explained to her students, "Girls and boys, we are now stopping Daily Five and going to lunch. When lunch and recess are over, we will join together again at the gathering place and continue with Daily Five." Because each work session stands alone as a thirty- to forty-five-minute period of independent and whole-group learning, students easily stop and quickly resume their work when they return.

We used to think that our literacy time had to be an extended, uninterrupted block. Rather, systematically teaching the behaviors of independence is what enables children to transfer their independence throughout the day, allowing the Daily Five to fit into the nooks and crannies of any schedule.

How do I build assessment into the Daily Five?

When we first began developing the Daily Five, we were constantly reflecting, wanting to make certain the children were learning. It felt as though the kids were not learning enough, because we couldn't "see" what they were learning, which traditionally meant something written on paper. We felt as though we weren't doing our jobs if our days did not include correcting something the kids had done, or having them fill out a form or respond to their Daily Five choices in some way. However, this type of work felt like unauthentic busywork that had no direct influence on their learning.

At the May 2001 Reading in the Content Areas conference in Seattle, Margaret Mooney said something that struck a chord with us: "Independence is synonymous with accountability." Our children deserve to be trusted to carry out our expectations and to accept the responsibility to do so. We don't need a daily paper to check. We see our children working, reading to themselves,

Figure 7-3 Joan assesses a student during the Daily Five.

and working on writing. We can hear them talking about their strategies and observe them putting those strategies into practice.

One of the advantages of the Daily Five is that the structure allows for uninterrupted blocks of time to work with children in a one-on-one situation. We use these work times to assess our children to inform our instruction.

When we know our children's strengths and greatest areas of need, we are able to diversify their instruction. These are the assessments we use in our classes:

- Anecdotal records
- Running records
- Developmental Reading Assessment
- Individual reading inventories

These assessments help us monitor children's growth by showing us what they have already learned and where they need to be nudged next. The ongoing assessments we do hold the most meaning for us. Each day as we meet with guided reading groups and then one on one with three to five students, we record this teaching and learning in our conferring notebooks. The notebooks become our diaries and documentation of where we have been with each student and our plans for where to go next, allowing for differentiated instruction for all of our students.

Three minutes seems sooo short for a practice session. Can't they be longer?

This is a question we frequently ask ourselves, and each year our answer is the same: it depends on our students. If children have never been introduced to the Daily Five, or if there are many behavior issues at the start, the practice sessions may need to be shorter, helping kids build their stamina a bit at a time. We always keep in mind that we don't want children to practice the behaviors of the Daily Five incorrectly, so building stamina slowly can help train their muscle memories the most desired way.

For classes that have used the Daily Five before, practice sessions can be longer. Students may be able to build their stamina more quickly, because their muscle memories have already been trained and quickly "remember" the correct behaviors.

How does my room arrangement affect the Daily Five?

Our current room arrangement includes areas such as the gathering place, the den (classroom library), small private work spaces, work spaces that can accommodate small groups of children, and open spaces for larger working groups. Once children are taught how to be independent in the variety of areas in the classroom, they have choice over where they spend their time during the day. Daily conversations involve topics such as "picking the best place for your brain and body to work," "where to do certain activities so as not to disturb others in our room," and "where can you be the best learner?"

Figure 7-4 Comfortable work spaces for the Daily Five might include cushions on the floor, tables, couches, carpeted areas, or lofts.

Being able to have children spread to all corners uses the room's total space. Giving children more private space facilitates independence because they are not sitting in one area of the room too close to good friends or adversaries.

I have such trouble when I confer with students—the other students are always interrupting or are distracted by my presence.

Conferring among our youngest or most distracted learners can be very disruptive to their learning and pull them off-task.

Once we have all components of the Daily Five up and running and are ready to begin conferring with children, we do a separate focus lesson. This lesson is geared toward teaching our youngest or highly distractible learners to stay focused and on-task even with a quiet conference happening nearby.

Ignoring the Teacher Focus Lesson

We start by reviewing what children have already learned. "Boys and girls, let's look at our I-charts. Now that you know how to be independent with all of the Daily Five, it is time for us to start our very important job. On the I-chart the student side shows all the things you do to be independent during Daily Five. On the teacher's side it shows what we do during Daily Five. We have a very important job—to teach students! This means that while you are working independently, we will be meeting with small groups and coming around to meet with individuals. Here's the trick: if we come to work with someone sitting near you, your job is to completely ignore us. We promise we will get a chance to meet with every single one of you this week, but when we are meeting with one of your friends nearby, you must pretend we are not even there. Let's practice this."

We then have children take their book boxes, get set up around the room, and begin working. We proceed to move slowly and quietly around the room, stopping to confer with individuals. We give particular attention to conferring near children we know to be highly distractible. This gives them a chance to practice staying focused and on-task, even with a conference taking place nearby.

Giving ample attention to this skill of "ignoring the teacher" sets the tone of the class for successful one-on-one conferring and independent work time.

Another strategy we use is to have two students designated each day as the classroom helpers, or "tech support." These students wear special vests, and their classmates know they need to go to them if their headphones aren't working, or if they need assistance with any materials. As the year goes on, these helpers tend to take the initiative to seek out and support students who need assistance with cleaning up supplies after Word Work, or replacing books on the shelf. Wearing the vest is a great concrete reminder of the responsibility and source of support for both the helpers and their classmates. When a student begins to distract us, we direct them to a classmate in a helper vest.

I have an odd number of students in my classroom. How do I handle Read to Someone and other partner tasks using elbow buddies that are essential for the Daily Five?

Once children check in, we count how many have selected Read to Someone. If the number is odd, we use three different methods to solve this dilemma.

1. Someone offers to switch out of Read to Someone, making a different choice to make the number even.
2. Someone offers to switch into Read to Someone, making the number even.
3. If no one is interested in switching, the odd person may read with a stuffed animal or hand puppet as his or her partner. This works best with primary students.

During our whole-group lessons we use elbow buddies. This strategy engages the whole class in synthesizing or practicing what has been taught. If an odd number of students exists in the whole-group lesson, a third person joins a partnership of two and adds his or her voice as well.

Some of the kids won't respond to the signal when it comes time to stop their Daily Five choice and come back to the gathering place.

One way we address this problem is by taking a look at how we are getting the class's attention. We use a strategy from Michael Grinder's book *ENvOY* called "Above, Pause, Whisper."

When we want to get the class's attention, such as when it is time for the end of a round of Daily Five, we use a chime or other unusual sound instead of our voices. We ring the chime, interrupting their work session and pausing long enough for even the kinesthetic children to look up. We then drop our voices below the level of the chimes to a whisper but keep them loud enough for the children to hear us. This causes them to look up to really hear what we are saying. We then ask them to join us in the gathering place. Hence the name Above (chime or other sound louder than our voices), Pause (standing very still, not moving, talking, or ringing the chime for a pregnant pause), and Whisper (the level of our voices giving the direction is quieter than the initial sound that got their attention).

This sounds like a subtle and perhaps insignificant change in the way we communicate to our class, but we are amazed each and every time at the results. We try to avoid using our voices to get their attention, instead saving them for teaching.

Sometimes this change in our approach of getting their attention and drawing them to the gathering place works for all the kids but one or two. At that point we quietly have a chat with those individuals. Often we find that they have a very specific reason for not wanting to join the rest of the class. We work hard to listen and understand their reasons, which have ranged from "I'm not done with what I am doing," to plain old "I don't want to change yet." Depending on the child, they may just need a reminder that they can pick up where they left off tomorrow during Daily Five.

We have found it important to make a note to help those students do just that the next day, because children often find picking up where they left off difficult. (It can be difficult for adults as well.) We will also teach the whole class this skill, showing them what it looks like when adults pick up where they left off the day or week before. Showing a class this skill involves focus lessons on rereading what we wrote yesterday so we can remember where we were, along with rereading the last paragraph or page in our books where we left off, stopping to remember what is happening in the story. Some students don't want to stop because they may be at a really great spot in the book they are reading or in the story they are writing. If this is really the case (and can't we always tell if that is really the case or just an avoidance strategy they are using?), we may tell them they can make the same choice again next round, after the focus lesson, so they can finish what they are reading or writing. We monitor this carefully, watching children's choices for patterns over time. We keep in mind that the research says children need to have extended practice reading *and* writing each day, but every once in a while, allowing children to do Read to Self or Work on Writing twice in a row can send a strong message saying, "I value you and your needs."

I have been using the Daily Five for weeks now, and some kids are still not independent.

There have been many years when we have had a child or two in our classes with more severe behavior challenges than others, and these behaviors may flare up during the Daily Five's independent work time.

Not having enough time to build muscle memory can lead to bothering others during work time. Along with lack of muscle memory, some children purposefully go off-task for attention. It doesn't matter which type of attention, negative or positive; it is merely attention they desire. Both of these reasons for off-task behavior can be addressed through more practice with the incorrect model/correct model approach.

In unusual and severe cases, we have had children who are absolutely not successful during independent work time. It seems that no amount of correct model, incorrect model, extra attention, or energy works. In cases such as these, we begin each day of the Daily Five in the same way.

1. Review the appropriate behaviors either as a whole group or with the individual child.
2. Let the child know right up front (oftentimes as part of a behavior plan) that we have a positive presupposition that he or she will be successful.
3. Have the child make an independent choice for the first work session of the Daily Five.
4. If the child is unable to be independent, we ask, "What is the goal for your behavior? Are you meeting that goal?" We try to have the child articulate this so he or she can begin to take responsibility for the behavior rather than us telling the child he or she isn't on-task, thereby owning the responsibility ourselves).
5. If the child isn't successful, he or she moves within close proximity of us.
6. After the next independent work choice check-in, we try again, following the same pattern as above.

Another strategy is to have the child practice for a few minutes at recess. This is not staying in as a punishment, detention, or missing their whole recess. Often these are the kids who need recess the most—we certainly don't want to keep them from running around on the playground! Practicing the behaviors you are trying to have them exhibit at recess takes place for two to three minutes. We work strictly on retraining their muscle memories and giving them positive feedback, filling their desire for attention.

I teach in a high-poverty area. I have a large number of English Language Learners this year, as well as transient students who are in our school only for a few weeks or months at a time. How can I make the Daily Five work for these students who come from such diverse backgrounds, or who have missed the training sessions that have established the routines?

As teachers, we are accustomed to "tweaking" things to fit the particular needs of our current situations and the children in our classes.

Our friend Pam, who teaches at a high-poverty school in our region, put it perfectly. She said, "I wouldn't change the teaching of Daily Five. What I would do differently is change how I approach each child every fall, or when they enroll in our school." She went on to say although she knew her school was meeting most of her class's basic needs for food and clothing, she wasn't prepared for the children's lack of trust and feeling safe with her when they first got to her classroom. "I tried to jump in the very first day teaching the independence of Daily Five, yet many of these children had gone three months being the primary caretaker for younger siblings, many of them not knowing where their next meal would come from. I needed to spend more time getting to know each child, listening to their stories, and building trust."

Trust and meeting basic human needs are a prerequisite to success with the Daily Five. Once those two conditions are met, teaching the Daily Five can go forward. Often the predictable routine of the Daily Five allows children to be successful and feel safe, even if their lives at home lack such safety and routines. Here is how we adjust our teaching to support children who lack support or stability in the home environment.

Room Arrangement

We begin each year by teaching children about our room arrangements, the many areas for learning, and how to choose where to sit. However, there are years when those arrangements need to start out differently to better meet the needs of our classes. Sometimes we have found it helpful to assign tables. Often these tables can be turned into "areas" where each Daily Five takes place. One table area is the Read-to-Self area, one the Read-to-Someone area, one the Work-on-Writing area, and so on. When introducing the Daily Five, this arrangement can provide students with more predictability and structure to help them feel safe. This structuring of room arrangement supports students as they gain locus of control so eventually the class can move to a more flexible room arrangement and seating choices.

Stamina

Building stamina looks different in each room every year. Some classes increase their stamina rapidly, whereas others may build their stamina by only ten to thirty seconds each day. There is no magic number of minutes or amount of time by which children can increase their stamina. We always let our students' behavior set the pace. Many years we have to remind ourselves that we have a totally new group of kids, and that they will not necessarily be on the same track to stamina as last year's kids.

Children Choosing the Order of Their Daily Five Components

Each time our friend Pam tried to move the children into choosing what they would read and write about, along with the order of their Daily Five choices, their behavior fell apart. As soon as the children moved into work time and Pam had gathered her first small group to teach, many of the other children would be up and moving, bothering others, getting drinks, and shopping for books—even though they had not shown these behaviors during the whole-group practice sessions.

As a way of working through this problem, Pam and many other teachers have found their most at-risk children have had great success when they are in charge of deciding what they read and the content of their writing, and the teacher facilitates the order in which they do the Daily Five. Supporting children with the order of their choices for a longer time into the school year helps them gain their locus of control. The ultimate goal is still to have children make choices over what they read, what they write, and the order in which they do the Daily Five.

Most At-Risk Students

Many years we have children who constantly struggle with staying focused, needing extra attention and extra individual instruction. When the Daily Five is up and running in our classrooms, we use the structure to give extra attention to those children.

We have the whole class check in, then call our small group for a focused lesson. While the small group gets set up, we quickly move to those most at-risk students to check in with them. It usually takes just a few seconds to have them reverbalize what they are working on this round and what their plan is, and to let them know we will touch base with them again after our small-group lesson. Letting kids know this right away can feed their need for attention and a bit of a focus. This can be all they need to get started and sustain independence.

Once the small group is finished and has moved back out to their Daily Five choices, we follow up on our most at-risk students. This helps them maintain their success in their own eyes and the eyes of the whole class, allowing that round of the Daily Five to go more smoothly and hence allowing all children to be more successful.

I teach fifth grade. How can I adapt the Daily Five for older students?

Many intermediate teachers, including middle school teachers, have asked us how this could work for them. We know the intermediate classroom schedule can be challenging, with additional subjects and shorter work periods. Teachers, parents, and students value the arts, so are willing to perform a bit of fancy scheduling that ensures time for each subject. As intermediate teachers we carve out forty-five to sixty minutes for reading and about the same for writing instruction and choose to integrate social studies and science into this literacy block.

Our primary classrooms most often have 90- to 120-minute blocks of time for literacy instruction. Intermediate classrooms have fewer blocks of time, so they may split up their reading and writing blocks. Pulling the writing and reading blocks apart can be and often is done, yet when our schedules allow, we keep them together, knowing this is optimum.

Read to Self, Read to Someone, and Work on Writing become the foundation for intermediate classes. We tend to leave Listen to Reading off the list because of the time constraint. This skill is usually addressed in the class read-aloud. But we have seen more social studies and science textbook publishers putting their books on CD so that children who can't access the text because of readability can listen and be part of the learning. When teachers have these CDs available and are integrating social studies or science, they find Listen to Reading to be a good strategy for their ELL or special education students.

We have taught all elementary grades from preschool through sixth grade. Students are students. We thought we couldn't teach sixth grade because the kids are so big, or kindergarten because the children are so small. We laugh now after loving kids of all ages, because the old adage "kids are kids" seems to ring true. All our students benefit from the explicit teaching and practicing of expected behaviors no matter what age.

With intermediate students we follow the same procedure for launching the Daily Five, but it's really only the Daily Three—Read to Self, Read to Someone, and Work on Writing. These are the independent behaviors we want children to know and act upon at any grade level. Depending on the class, older children can usually start with more than a three-minute practice. Instead they might start with five to six minutes. In the fall, even intermediate students need to build their stamina to sit and read after a summer of fun. So do we, for that matter!

BIBLIOGRAPHY

■■■■■

Allen, Janet. 2000. *Yellow Brick Roads: Shared and Guided Paths to Independent Reading 4–12.* Portland, ME: Stenhouse.

Allington, Richard. 2001. *What Really Matters for Struggling Readers: Designing Research-Based Programs.* New York: Addison-Wesley Longman.

Allington, Richard and Peter Johnston. 2002. *Reading to Learn: Lessons From Exemplary Fourth-Grade Classrooms.* New York: Guilford Press.

Alvermann, Donna and Stephen Phelps. 2002. *Content Reading and Literacy: Succeeding in Today's Diverse Classrooms.* Boston: Allyn and Bacon.

Anderson, Richard. 1985. *Becoming a Nation of Readers: The Report of the Commission on Reading.* National Academy of Education, National Institute of Education and the Center for the Study of Reading. Pittsburg, PA.

Atwell, Nancie. 1987. *In the Middle: Writing, Reading, and Learning with Adolescents.* Portsmouth, NH: Heinemann.

Baker, Keith. 1994. *Big Fat Hen.* San Diego: Red Wagon Books.

Beaver, Joetta. 1997. *Developmental Reading Assessment (DRA).* Parsippany, NJ: Pearson Education.

Betts, Emmett. 1946. *Foundations of Reading Instruction.* New York: American Book Co.

Bridges, William. 2003. *Managing Transitions: Making the Most of Change.* Cambridge, MA: Da Capo Press.

Buckner, Aimee. 2005. *Notebook Know-How: Strategies for the Writer's Notebook.* Portland, ME: Stenhouse.

Burnes, Paul and Betty Roe. 2002. *Informal Reading Inventory: Preprimer to Twelfth Grade.* Boston: Houghton Mifflin.

Cambourne, Brian and J. Turbill. 1987. *Coping with Chaos.* Portsmouth, NH: Heinemann.

Coulton, Mia. 2001. *Look at Danny.* Beachwood, OH: Mary Ruth Books.

DiCamillo, Kate and Timothy B. Ering. 2003. *The Tale of Despereaux.* Cambridge, MA: Candlewick.

Ekwall, Eldon and James Shanker. 1999. *Ekwall/Shanker Reading Inventory.* Boston: Allyn and Bacon.

Fletcher, Ralph and JoAnn Portalupi. 1998. *Craft Lessons: Teaching Writing K–8.* Portland, ME: Stenhouse.

Fountas, Irene and Gay Su Pinnell. 2001. *Guiding Readers and Writers Grade 3–6: Teaching Comprehension, Genre, and Content Literacy.* Portsmouth, NH: Heinemann.

Gambrell, L. B., R. M. Wilson and W. N. Gantt. 1981. "Classroom Observations of Task-Attending Behaviors of Good and Poor Readers." *Journal of Educational Research* 74(6): 400–404.

Gentry, Richard. 2004. *The Science of Spelling: The Explicit Specifics That Make Great Readers and Writers (and Spellers!)* Portsmouth, NH: Heinemann.

Graves, Donald. 1985. "All Children Can Write." *Learning Disabilities Focus* 1(1): 36–43.

Grinder, Michael. 1991. *Righting the Educational Conveyor Belt.* Portland, OR: Metamorphous Press.

———. 1995. *ENVoY: Your Personal Guide to Classroom Management.* Battle Ground, WA: Michael Grinder and Associates.

Harvey, Stephanie and Anne Goudvis. 2000. *Strategies That Work: Teaching Comprehension to Enhance Understanding.* Portland, ME: Stenhouse.

Healy, Jane. 1994. *Your Child's Growing Mind; A Practical Guide to Brain Development and Learning From Birth to Adolescence.* New York: Doubleday.

Henkes, Kevin. 1996. *Lilly's Purple Plastic Purse.* New York: Greenwillow Books.

Hoban, Tana. 1997. *Look.* New York: Greenwillow Books.

Hopkins, Gary. 2002. Character(istics) Count!—What Principals Look for When Hiring New Teachers. Education World. http://www.educationworld.com/.

Kame'enui, Edward J., Douglas W. Carnine, Robert C. Dixon, Deborah C. Simmons and Michael D. Coyne. 2002. *Effective Teaching Strategies That Accommodate Diverse Learners.* Columbus, OH: Merrill Prentice Hall.

Katz, Alan and David Catrow. 2001. *Take Me Out of the Bathtub and Other Silly Dilly Songs.* New York: Margaret K. McElderry Books.

Krashen, Stephen. 2004. *The Power of Reading: Insights from the Research.* Portsmouth, NH: Heinemann.

Layne, Steven. 2001. *This Side of Paradise.* Gretna, LA: Pelican Publishing.

Leinhardt, Gaea and A. Pallay. 1982. "Prestrictive Educational Settings: Exile or Haven?" *Review of Educational Research* 524: 557–578.

Leinhardt, Gaea, Naomi Zigmond, and William Cooley. 1981. "Reading Instruction and Its Effects." *American Educational Research Journal* 18(3): 343–361.

Marshall, J. C. 2000. *Are They Really Reading?* Portland, ME: Stenhouse Publishers.

Marten, Cindy. 2003. *Word Crafting: Teaching Spelling, Grades K–6.* Portsmouth, NH: Heinemann.

Miller, Debbie. 2002. *Reading with Meaning: Teaching Comprehension in the Primary Grades.* Portland, ME: Stenhouse.

Mooney, Margaret. 1990. *Reading To, With and By Children.* Katonah, NY: Richard C. Owen.

Morrow, Lesley Mandel, Linda Gambrell and Michael Pressley. 2003. *Best Practices in Literacy Instruction.* New York: Guilford Press.

Osborne, Mary Pope. 2003. *Haunted Castle on Hallow's Eve.* Magic Tree House 30. New York: Random House.

Nesbitt, Kenn. 2001. *The Aliens Have Landed.* Minnetonka, MN: Meadowbrook.

Park, Barbara. 2000. *Junie B. Jones Has a Peep in Her Pocket.* New York: Random House.

———. 2003. *Junie B., First Grader: Toothless Wonder.* New York: Random House.

Pearson, P. David, and M. C. Gallagher. 1983. "The Instruction of Reading Comprehension." *Contemporary Educational Psychology* 8: 317–344.

Pilgreen, Janice. 2000. *The SSR Handbook: How to Organize and Manage a Sustained Silent Reading Program.* Portsmouth, NH: Heinemann.

Pressley, Michael, Richard Allington, Ruth Wharton-McDonald, Cathy Collins Block and Lesley Mandel Morrow. 2001. *Learning to Read: Lessons from Exemplary First-Grade Classrooms.* New York: Guilford Press.

Routman, Regie. 2003. *Reading Essentials: The Specifics You Need to Teach Reading Well.* Portsmouth, NH: Heinemann.

———. 2005. *Writing Essentials: Raising Expectations and Results While Simplifying Teaching.* Portsmouth, NH: Heinemann.

Sibberson, Franki and Karen Szymusiak. 2003. *Still Learning to Read: Teaching Students in Grades 3–6.* Portland, ME: Stenhouse.

Shannon, David. 1998. *No, David!* New York: Blue Sky Press.

Shaywitz, Sally, M.D. 2003. *Overcoming Dyslexia.* New York: Alfred Knopf.

Snowball, Diane and Faye Bolton. 1999. *Spelling K–8: Planning and Teaching.* Portland, ME: Stenhouse.

Stahl, S. A. 2004. "What Do We Know About Fluency?" In P. McCordle and V. Chhabra, eds., *The Voice of Evidence in Reading Research,* pp. 187–211. Baltimore: Brookes.

Seuss, Dr. 1957. *The Cat in the Hat.* New York: Random House.

Tovani, Cris. 2000. *I Read It, but I Don't Get It: Comprehension Strategies for Adolescent Readers.* Portland, ME: Stenhouse.

Trelease, Jim. 2001. *The Read-Aloud Handbook.* New York: Penguin Books.

Wexo, John Bonnett. 2000. *Rhinos.* Zoo Book 2. Chanhassen, MN: Child's World.

Willems, Mo. 2003. *Don't Let the Pigeon Drive the Bus.* New York: Hyperion Books.

APPENDIX

■■■■■

Read to Self
Day One Launching Chart

Teaching Actions	Student Behaviors	Materials
Setting Purpose for the Day Sense of Urgency for Read to Self	Become a better reader. It is fun. Practice skills.	
Focus Lesson Three ways to read a book Choose a story and read it three different ways. Read the pictures. Read the words.	Listen to story.	Picture book
Brainstorm Read-to-Self Behaviors Behaviors and ideas are made visual by writing them on an I-chart. 　　　　Read to Self Student　　　　Teacher	Discuss and brainstorm Read-to-Self behaviors.	Chart paper
Correct Model	One to three students model the appropriate Read-to-Self behaviors in front of whole class.	Book box or reading material
Incorrect Model	One or two students model the inappropriate Read-to-Self behaviors in front of whole class, then model correct behaviors.	Book box or reading material
Building Stamina—3-Minute Practice Teacher stays out of the way of children's reading. No eye contact or managing by proximity at this time. Teacher may practice sitting at guided reading or assessment spot.	Children, with their book boxes, are placed around the room. Students practice Read to Self for 3 minutes.	Designated spaces around the room that are comfortable (e.g., under tables, carpeted reading nooks, couches, pillows)

Read to Self
Day One Launching Chart (continued)

Teaching Actions	Student Behaviors	Materials
Signal and Check In Teacher signals for students to return to the whole group.	Check in—How did it go? Review anchor chart.	Chimes, lights, or bell
Model Again	One or two students model appropriate and inappropriate behaviors, always ending with appropriate behaviors.	Book box or reading material
Building Stamina— 3-Minute Practice	Repeat 3-minute practice.	Designated spaces around the room that are comfortable (e.g., under tables, carpeted reading nooks, couches, pillows)
Signal and Check In Teacher signals for students to return to whole group.	Check in—How did it go? Review anchor chart.	Chimes, lights, or bell
Closure **Review the Lesson.**	What did we learn?	I-chart

Read to Someone
Launching Chart

Teacher Actions	Learning Behaviors	Materials
Setting Purpose for the Day Sense of Urgency for Read to Someone	Become a better reader. Work on fluency. Practice skills It is fun.	
Focus Lesson How to sit—EEKK Check for understanding	Model with students EEKK— Elbow, Elbow, Knee, Knee. I just heard you read . . . (who, what).	Partners Partners and "check mark" (optional)
Brainstorm Read-to-Someone Behaviors Behaviors and ideas are made visual by writing them on an I-chart. Read to Someone Independence Student Teacher	Discuss and review behaviors.	Chart paper

Read to Someone
Launching Chart (continued)

Teacher Actions	Learning Behaviors	Materials
Correct Model	One to three students model the appropriate Read-to-Someone behaviors in front of whole class.	Book box or reading material and partners
Incorrect Model	One or two students model the inappropriate Read-to-Someone behaviors in front of whole class, then model correct behaviors.	Book box or reading material and partners
Building Stamina— 3-Minute Practice Teacher stays out of the way of children's reading. No eye contact or managing by proximity at this time. Teacher may practice sitting at guided reading or assessment spot.	Students practice Read to Someone for 3 minutes.	Designated spaces around the room that are comfortable (e.g., under tables, carpeted reading nooks, couches, pillows)
Signal and Check In Teacher signals for students to return to the whole group.	Students return to gathering place and check in—How did it go? Review I-chart for Read to Someone, behaviors of EEKK, and Check for Understanding.	Chimes, lights, or bell
Model Again	One or two students model appropriate and inappropriate behaviors, always ending with appropriate behaviors.	Book box or reading material and partner
Building Stamina– 3-Minute Practice	Repeat 3-minute practice.	Designated spaces around the room that are comfortable (e.g., under tables, carpeted reading nooks, couches, pillows)
Signal and Check In Teacher signals for students to return to whole group.	Check in—How did it go? Review I-chart for Read-to-Someone and behaviors of EEKK and check for understanding.	Chimes, lights, or bell
Closure **Review the Lesson.**	What did we learn?	I-chart

Listen to Reading
Launching Chart

Teaching Actions	Student Behaviors	Materials
Setting Purpose for the Day **Sense of Urgency for Listen to Reading**	Become a better reader. Learn and understand new words and stories. It is fun.	
Focus Lesson Materials setup Listening and following along with words or pictures	Model with students how to locate tape and book, and use the recorder. Model following the picture or following the words with finger or bookmark.	Book Tape/CD Tape player or CD player Computer
Brainstorm Behaviors and ideas are made visual by writing them on an I-chart. Listen to Reading Independence Student Teacher	Discuss and brainstorm Listen-to-Reading behaviors.	Chart paper
Correct Model	One to three students model the appropriate Listen-to-Reading behaviors in front of whole class.	Book Tape/CD Tape player or CD player Computer
Incorrect Model	One or two students model the inappropriate Listen-to-Reading behaviors in front of whole class, then model correct behaviors.	Book Tape/CD Tape player or CD player Computer
Building Stamina— Practice Teacher stays out of the way of children's reading. No eye contact or managing by proximity at this time. Teacher may practice sitting at guided reading or assessment spot.	A few students practice Listen to Reading. Because this is engaging, students will have much more stamina to stick with this task right from the start. Other students are working on other Daily Five choices.	Book Tape/CD Tape player or CD player Computer
Signal and Check In	Teacher signals for students to return to the whole group. Check in—How did it go? Review anchor chart.	Chimes, lights, or bell

Listen to Reading
Launching Chart (continued)

Teaching Actions	Student Behaviors	Materials
Model Again if Time Allows.	One or two students model appropriate and inappropriate behaviors, always ending with appropriate behaviors.	Book Tape/CD Tape player or CD player Computer
Building Stamina—Practice	This second practice allows more students to try Listen to Reading on this first day.	Book Tape/CD Tape player or CD player Computer
Signal and Check In Teacher signals for students to return to whole group.	Students return to gathering place. Check in—How did it go? Review I-chart for Listen to Reading. Review other I-charts if necessary.	Chimes, lights, or bell
Closure **Review the Lesson.**	What did we learn?	I-chart for Listen to Reading or the other Daily Five behaviors

Work on Writing
Launching Chart

Teaching Behaviors	Learning Behaviors	Materials
Setting Purpose for the Day **Sense of Urgency for Work on Writing**	Become a better reader and writer. We care about writing and the people who read it. Choice of what to write about It is fun.	
Focus Lesson How to write words you can't spell	Model writing, showing what to do during writing when you can't spell words—underline and go on.	Notebook Pencil/pen Chart paper

Work on Writing
Launching Chart (continued)

Teaching Behaviors	Learning Behaviors	Materials
Brainstorm Work-on-Writing Behaviors Work on Writing Independence Student Teacher	Write student responses on I-chart	Chart paper
Correct Model	One to three students model the appropriate Work-on-Writing behaviors in front of whole class.	Notebook Pencil/pen
Incorrect Model	One or two students model the inappropriate Work-on-Writing behaviors in front of whole class, then model correct behaviors.	Notebook Pencil/pen
Building Stamina—Practice Teacher stays out of the way of children's reading. No eye contact or managing by proximity at this time. Teacher may practice sitting at guided reading or assessment spot.	Students practice Work on Writing for 3 minutes.	Notebook Pencil/pen
Signal and Check In	Teacher signals for students to return to the whole group. Check in—How did it go? Review I-chart.	Chimes, lights, or bell
Model Again if Time Allows.	One or two students model appropriate and inappropriate behaviors, always ending with appropriate behaviors.	Notebook Pencil/pen
Building Stamina—Practice	This second practice allows students to build stamina.	Notebook Pencil/pen
Signal and Check In	Teacher signals for students to return to whole group. Check in—How did it go? Review I-chart.	Chimes, lights, or bell
Closure **Review the Lesson.**	What did we learn?	Anchor chart

Word Work
Day One Launching Chart

Teacher Actions	Learning Behaviors	Materials
Sense of Urgency for Word Work	We care about our writing and the people who will read it. Helps us become better readers, writers, and spellers. It is fun.	
Focus Lesson Introduce procedures for materials setup, exploration, and cleanup.	Students watch and listen while materials are being presented.	Whiteboards Magnetic letters Wikki Stix Clay Letter stamps Colored markers
Brainstorm Word-Work Behaviors Behaviors and ideas are made visual by writing them on an I-chart. Word Work Materials setup Student Teacher	Discuss behaviors for materials setup. ■ One person takes out materials of his or her choice. ■ Same person sets up materials in a quiet location. ■ Stay in one spot until time to return materials.	Chart paper
Correct Model	One to three students model the appropriate material setup and exploration behaviors in front of whole class.	Whiteboards Magnetic letters Wikki Stix Clay Letter stamps Colored markers
Incorrect Model	One or two students model inappropriate materials setup and exploration behaviors in front of whole class then model correct behaviors.	Whiteboards Magnetic letters Wikki Stix Clay Letter stamps Colored markers
Building Stamina— 3–7-Minute Practice Teacher stays out of the way of children's practice. No eye contact or managing by proximity at this time. Teacher may practice sitting at guided reading or assessment spot.	Students practice materials setup and exploration for 3–7 minutes.	Designated spaces around the room that are comfortable (e.g., under tables, carpeted reading nooks, couches, pillows)

Word Work
Day One Launching Chart (continued)

Teacher Actions	Learning Behaviors	Materials
Signal and Check In Teacher signals for students to return to the whole group.	Students return to gathering place and check in—How did it go? Review I-chart of materials setup.	Chimes, lights, or bell
Brainstorm Behaviors Brainstorm I-chart of cleanup behaviors and routines. Word Work Materials cleanup Student Teacher	Discuss cleanup behaviors.	Chart paper
Correct Model	One to three students model the appropriate material cleanup behaviors and routines in front of whole class.	Whiteboards Magnetic letters Wikki Stix Clay Letter stamps Colored markers
Signal and Check In Teacher signals for students to return to whole group.	Students return to gathering place and check in—How did it go? Review I-chart.	Chimes, lights, or bell
Closure **Review the Lesson.**	What did we learn?	I-chart

Launching the Daily Five
The First Five Weeks

Day 1

Focus Lesson

Make anchor chart: "Three Ways to Read a Book."
Read pictures.
Read words.
Model first two ways to read a book. See page 47.

Read to Self

Begin teaching "10 steps to Improve Muscle Memory" See page 37.
Also see launching chart for Read to Self, page 111

Closure, sharing, and review of the lessons of the day

Day 2

Focus Lesson

Review 2 ways to read a book and model third way—"Retell a familiar text." See page 47.

Read to Self

Review I-chart.
Continue "10 Steps to Improve Muscle Memory," adding 1–2 minutes to stamina.

Closure, sharing, and review of the lessons of the day

Day 3

Focus Lesson

Create an I-chart to teach and reinforce "Where to Sit in Room."
1-minute review of "Three Ways to Read a Book."

Read to Self

Review I-chart.
Continue "10 Steps to Improve Muscle Memory," adding 1–2 minutes to stamina.

Closure, sharing, and review of the lessons of the day

Day 4

Focus Lesson

Review I-chart "Where to Sit in Room," practice again.
One-minute review of "Three Ways to Read a Book"

Read to Self

Review I-chart.
Continue "10 Steps to Improve Muscle Memory," adding 1–2 minutes to stamina.

Closure, sharing, and review of the lessons of the day

Day 5

Focus Lesson

Quick review of anchor charts and I-charts from each day:
Three Ways to Read a Book
Where to Sit in Room
Read-to-Self Behaviors

Read to Self

"10 Steps to Improve Muscle Memory," adding 1–2 minutes to stamina.

Closure, sharing, and review of the lessons of the day

Writing

In your modeled writing, demonstrate "underlining words you are not sure how to spell."

= Introduced that day

Day 6

Focus Lesson

Teach how to choose good-fit books." See good-fit-books lesson, page 29.

Read to Self

Quick review of Read-to-Self chart
Continue to use "10 Steps to Improve Muscle Memory," adding 1–2 minutes to stamina.

Work on Writing
Focus Lesson

Introduce Work on Writing. Use "10 Steps to Improve Muscle Memory." See page 37. See Work on Writing launching chart, page 115.

Closure, sharing, and review of the lessons of the day

Launching the Daily Five
The First Five Weeks (continued)

Day 7	*Day 8*	*Day 9*
Focus Lesson Quick review of "Choosing Good-Fit Books" chart	**Focus Lesson** Quick review of "Choosing Good-Fit Books" chart	**Focus Lesson** Quick review of "Choosing Good-Fit Books" chart
Read to Self Quick review of Read-to-Self I-chart Continue building stamina and developing independence.	**Read to Self** Quick review of Read-to-Self I-chart Continue building stamina and developing independence.	**Read to Self** Quick review of Read-to-Self I-chart Continue building stamina and developing independence.
Work on Writing Review Work-on-Writing I-chart. Use "10 Steps to Improve Muscle Memory," adding 1–2 minutes to stamina. See page 37.	**Work on Writing Focus Lesson** Create I-chart for where to sit in room during Work on Writing. Review Work-on-Writing I-chart. Continue building stamina and developing independence.	**Work on Writing Focus Lesson** Brainstorm a list of topics children could write about. Then students write their own. Also see **Notebook Know-How** by Amy Buckner for ideas. Review Work-on-Writing I-chart. Continue building stamina and developing independence.
Closure, sharing, and review of the lessons of the day	**Closure, sharing, and review of the lessons of the day**	**Closure, sharing, and review of the lessons of the day**

= Introduced that day

Launching the Daily Five
The First Five Weeks (continued)

Day 10	*Day 11*	*Day 12*
Focus Lesson Quick review of "Choosing Good-Fit Books" chart	**Focus Lesson 1** Quick review of charts	**Focus Lesson 1** Quick review of charts
Read to Self Quick review of Read-to-Self I-chart Continue building stamina and developing independence.	**Read to Self** Continue building stamina and developing independence.	**Read to Self** Continue building stamina and developing independence.
Work on Writing **Focus Lesson** Brainstorm a list of forms children could write about (letters, lists, narratives, expository, etc.). Then students write their own. Review Work-on-Writing I-chart. Continue building stamina and developing independence.	**Focus Lesson 2** Begin district or state writing curriculum for focus lessons. These lessons are skills and/or strategies all of your students need.	**Focus Lesson 2** Continue district or state writing curriculum for focus lessons.
Closure, sharing, and review of the lessons of the day	**Work on Writing** Continue building stamina and developing independence.	**Work on Writing** Continue building stamina and developing independence.
	Focus Lessons 3 Review how to sit during partner reading (EEKK). See page 63. Model and practice Check for Understanding. See page 64.	**Focus Lesson 3** Model and practice how partners read using the same book: "I heard you read . . ." See page 64.
	Read to Someone Introduce Read to Someone using "10 Steps to Independence." See page 37. Also see launching chart for Read to Someone, page 112.	**Read to Someone** Continue building stamina and developing independence.
	Closure, sharing, and review of the lessons of the day	**Closure, sharing, and review of the lessons of the day**

 = Introduced that day

Launching the Daily Five
The First Five Weeks (continued)

Day 13	Day 14	Day 15
Focus Lesson 1 Quick review of charts	**Focus Lesson 1** Quick review of charts	**Focus Lesson 1** Quick review of charts
Read to Self Continue building stamina and developing independence.	**Read to Self** Continue building stamina and developing independence.	**Read to Self** Continue building stamina and developing independence.
Focus Lesson 2 Continue district or state writing curriculum for focus lessons.	**Focus Lesson 2** Continue district or state writing curriculum for focus lessons.	**Focus Lesson 2** Continue district or state writing curriculum for focus lessons.
Work on Writing Continue building stamina and developing independence.	**Work on Writing** Continue building stamina and developing independence.	**Work on Writing** Continue building stamina and developing independence.
Focus Lesson 3 Model and practice how partners read two different books. See page 69.	**Focus Lesson 3** Brainstorm and practice "How to Choose Books." *Let's Make a Deal *Rock, Paper, Scissors (See page 70)	**Focus Lesson 3** Create I-chart for where to sit in room during Read to Someone. See page 70.
Read to Someone Continue building stamina and developing independence.	**Read to Someone** Continue building stamina and developing independence.	**Read to Someone** Continue building stamina and developing independence.
Closure, sharing, and review of the lessons of the day	**Closure, sharing, and review of the lessons of the day**	**Closure, sharing, and review of the lessons of the day**

= Introduced that day

Launching the Daily Five
The First Five Weeks (continued)

Day 16	*Day 17*	*Day 18*
Focus Lesson 1 Quick review of charts Start transitioning from teaching Read-to-Self behaviors to teaching reading lesson.	**Focus Lesson 1** Quick review of charts Teach reading lesson.	**Focus Lesson 1** Quick review of charts Teach reading lesson.
Read to Self Continue building stamina and developing independence.	**Read to Self** Continue building stamina and developing independence.	**Read to Self** Continue building stamina and developing independence.
Focus Lesson 2 Start transitioning from teaching writing behaviors to writing lessons.	**Focus Lesson 2** Quick review of charts Teach writing lesson.	**Focus Lesson 2** Quick review of charts Teach writing lesson.
Work on Writing Continue building stamina and developing independence.	**Work on Writing** Continue building stamina and developing independence.	**Work on Writing** Continue building stamina and developing independence.
Focus Lesson 3 Quick review of charts Model and practice "How to Choose a Partner." Create I-chart. See page 71	**Focus Lesson 3** Quick review of charts Model and practice "Coaching or Time." See page 73	**Focus Lesson 3** Quick review of charts Model and practice "Coaching or Time."
Read to Someone Continue building stamina and developing independence.	**Read to Someone** Continue building stamina and developing independence.	**Read to Someone** Continue building stamina and developing independence.
Closure, sharing, and review of the lessons of the day	**Closure, sharing, and review of the lessons of the day**	**Closure, sharing, and review of the lessons of the day**

= Introduced that day

Launching the Daily Five
The First Five Weeks (continued)

Day 19	Day 20	Day 21
Focus Lesson 1 Quick review of charts Teach reading lesson.	**Focus Lesson 1** Quick review of charts Teach reading lesson.	**Focus Lesson 1** Quick review of charts Teach reading lesson.
Read to Self Continue building stamina and developing independence.	**Read to Self** Continue building stamina and developing independence.	**Read to Self** Continue building stamina and developing independence.
Focus Lesson 2 Quick review of charts Teach writing lesson.	**Focus Lesson 2** Quick review of charts Teach writing lesson.	**Focus Lesson 2** Quick review of charts Teach writing lesson.
Work on Writing Continue building stamina and developing independence.	**Work on Writing** Continue building stamina and developing independence.	**Work on Writing** Continue building stamina and developing independence.
Focus Lesson 3 Quick review of charts Model and practice "Coaching or Time."	**Focus Lesson 3** Quick review of charts Start transitioning from teaching Read-to-Someone behaviors to teaching reading lessons.	**Focus Lesson 3** Quick review of charts Teach reading lesson.
Read to Someone Continue building stamina and developing independence.	**Read to Someone** Continue building stamina and developing independence.	**Read to Someone** Continue building stamina and developing independence.
Focus Lesson 4 Brainstorm anchor chart for how to **set up** and **cleanup** materials for Word Work and material placement. See Word-Work launching chart, page 117.	**Focus Lesson 4** Quick review of charts Model setup and cleanup for Word Work.	**Focus Lesson 4** Quick review of charts Model setup and cleanup for Word Work.
Word Work Introduce Word Work. Use "10 Steps to Improve Muscle Memory." See page 37. See launching chart for Word Work, page 117.	**Word Work** Continue building stamina and developing independence.	**Word Work** Continue building stamina and developing independence.
Closure, sharing, and review of the lessons of the day	**Closure, sharing, and review of the lessons of the day**	**Closure, sharing, and review of the lessons of the day**

= Introduced that day

Launching the Daily Five
The First Five Weeks (continued)

Day 22	*Day 23*
Focus Lesson 1 Quick review of charts Teach reading lesson.	**Focus Lesson 1** Quick review of charts Teach reading lesson.
Read to Self Continue building stamina and developing independence.	**Read to Self** Continue building stamina and developing independence.
Focus Lesson 2 Quick review of charts Teach writing lesson.	**Focus Lesson 2** Quick review of charts Teach writing lesson.
Work on Writing Continue building stamina and developing independence.	**Work on Writing** Continue building stamina and developing independence.
Focus Lesson 3 Quick review of charts Teach reading lesson.	**Focus Lesson 3** Quick review of charts Teach reading lesson.
Read to Someone Continue building stamina and developing independence.	**Read to Someone** Continue building stamina and developing independence.
Focus Lesson 4 Quick review of charts Model setup and cleanup for Word Work.	**Focus Lesson 4** Quick review of charts Model setup and cleanup for Word Work.
Word Work Continue building stamina and developing independence.	**Word Work** Continue building stamina and developing independence.
Listen to Reading Introduce Listen to Reading. Use "10 Steps to Improve Muscle Memory." See page 37. See launching chart for Listen to Reading on page 115. A few students practice at once. Because most classrooms have a limited supply of listening equipment, this Daily Five is never practiced with all students at the same time.	**Listen to Reading** Continue building stamina and developing independence a few students at a time.
Closure, sharing, and review of the lessons of the day	**Closure, sharing, and review of the lessons of the day**

= Introduced that day

**Launching the Daily Five
The First Five Weeks** (continued)

Day 24

Focus Lesson 1
Teach reading lesson.
Blend the Daily Five together.
Students have a choice over which Daily to do first, second, third, fourth, and fifth. Review I-charts. Teach children how to check in. See page 93.

Student Independent Work 1
Children are reading, writing, partner reading, doing Word Work, and/or listening to reading, continuing to build stamina and develop independence.

Focus Lesson 2
Teach writing lesson.
Continue to teach children how to check in. This session children choose a different daily from their first session.

Student Independent Work 2
Children are reading, writing, partner reading, doing Word Work, and/or listening to reading, continuing to build stamina and develop independence.

Focus Lesson 3
Teach reading lesson.
Continue to teach children how to check in. This session children choose a different task from their previous sessions.

Student Independent Work 3
Children are reading, writing, partner reading, doing Word Work, and/or listening to reading, continuing to build stamina and develop independence.

Focus Lesson 4
Teach a Word-Work lesson.
Continue to teach children how to check in. This session children choose a different task from their previous sessions.

Student Independent Work 4
Children are reading, writing, partner reading, doing Word Work, and/or listening to reading, continuing to build stamina and develop independence.

Closure, sharing, and review of the lessons of the day

*If you have time for only 2 student independent work sessions, children choose between the Daily Five, participating in only two.
*If you have time for only 3 student independent work sessions, the same is true: they have choice.

Day 25

Focus Lesson 1
Teach reading lesson.

Student Independent Work 1
Children are reading, writing, partner reading, doing Word Work, and/or listening to reading.

Focus Lesson 2
Teach writing lesson.

Student Independent Work 2
Children are reading, writing, partner reading, doing Word Work, and/or listening to reading.

Focus Lesson 3
Teach a reading lesson.

Student Independent Work 3
Children are reading, writing, partner reading, doing Word Work, and/or listening to reading.

Focus Lesson 4
Teach a Word-Work lesson.

Student Independent Work 4
Children are reading, writing, partner reading, doing Word Work, and/or listening to reading.

Closure, sharing, and review of the lessons of the day

At this time all of the Daily Five have been introduced, practiced and refined. Stamina may continue to be built if needed. The structure is set up for the remainder of the year.

= Introduced that day